Marvels of
Math

Marvels of Math

Fascinating Reads and Awesome Activities

Kendall Haven

1998
Teacher Ideas Press
A Division of
Libraries Unlimited, Inc.
Englewood, Colorado

*To every person who has found joy and intrigue
in a math puzzle, and to every mind who ever
gazed with wonder and curiosity at our system of
numbers and math.*

ᵔᵔᵔ

TEACHER IDEAS PRESS
A Division of
Libraries Unlimited, Inc.
P.O. Box 6633
Englewood, CO 80155-6633
1-800-237-6124
www.lu.com/tip

Production Editor: Kevin W. Perizzolo
Copy Editor: Curtis D. Holmes
Proofreader: Susie Sigman
Indexer: Lee Brower
Typesetter: Kay Minnis

Library of Congress Cataloging-in-Publication Data

Haven, Kendall F.
    Marvels of math : fascinating reads and awesome activities /
by Kendall Haven.
    xii, 172 p. 17x25 cm.
    Includes bibliographical references and index.
    ISBN 1-56308-585-2 (pbk.)
    1. Mathematics--History. 2. Mathematics--Miscellanea.   I. Title.
QA21.H32   1998
510--dc21
                                                        98-34084
                                                            CIP

Contents

Infinity . . . and Beyond!

Stories
About Geometry

Elementary Elements

"Flying" High

Shadow Boxing

Stories About
Mathematical Concepts

The Weighing Game

Stories About
Calculating Machines

Introduction

We tend to view math as either an interesting game to play, or an endless maze of rote memorization, unintelligible rules and theorems, and mind-numbing equations stuffed with incomprehensible symbols.

I have heard middle school students groan, "Where'd this stuff come from?" When I have asked where they thought it came from, the general answer is that our current set of real and complex numbers and the full range of arithmetic, algebra, geometry, trigonometry, and calculus have always been here. It's as if the Big Bang created both expanding hydrogen and helium particles *and* the numbers and math processes to describe and analyze them. They feel that mathematics is a rigid, unfriendly system that has existed inalterably throughout all time.

They couldn't be more mistaken. Mathematics has evolved to meet specific human problem-solving needs. People created every bit of our number and math systems. They *invented* it. They created the math that they needed to solve everyday, practical problems, and to describe everyday, real-world phenomena—from the first invention of whole numbers to describe the members of groups (the number of sheep in a pen, saber-tooth tigers on the hunt, or mouths to feed at dinner) to the recent development of chaos theory and surreal numbers.

All of math was not invented back in dim-dark ancient history. Roman numerals do not have a zero, and neither did the Greek letter-based system for representing numbers. Zero was first recognized as a number in AD 800.

It wasn't until the thirteenth century that most of Europe accepted, and began to use, the Arabic number system and zero. As late as the fourteenth century, many cultures didn't acknowledge the existence of negative numbers, claiming—as did the mighty Greeks—that it was impossible to have less than nothing. Complex numbers weren't created until the sixteenth century.

Even more exciting, new math concepts and approaches are *still* being discovered and invented. For example, surreal numbers, a nifty way to count beyond infinity, were invented in 1992. Much of the math learned over your lifetime is less than one hundred years old. Likely as not, some math that you will learn and use has not yet been created!

The history of math is a process of cumulative effort and sudden insight. We tend to give all the credit to the one individual who fit the final piece into the puzzle and saw the whole picture. But that "discovery" was no grander than countless other necessary but unnoticed steps that came before—often from unidentified mathematicians.

For example, Newton is credited with creating our system of calculus. But Liebnitz in Germany simultaneously and independently developed a very similar system. Fermat, Cardano, Huygens, and many others developed math procedures that *almost* count as calculus. Even Aristotle used very small (if not infinitesimal) increments to make computations. The credit for developing calculus should rightfully go to a hundred mathematicians spread over a dozen centuries. But Newton, the first one to put the final pieces together, gets the credit.

Besides misunderstanding how mathematics came to be, most people fail to recognize what it is. Math is a language, a language used by science. Math is really a short-hand version of English. For example, $A = \pi r^2$, the formula for the area of a circle, really means "the amount of area inside a circle can be found by multiplying π (a mathematical constant equal to the ratio of the distance around a circle to the distance straight across) times the distance from the center of the circle to the outer edge and times that same distance once again." The formula is so much shorter and easier to write than the English. You just have to learn the math language.

To understand math, first treat it as a foreign language and learn to translate each symbol and term into English. *Then* learn what the various operations mean and how to perform them.

More than in other fields, math development is a group effort, riding on the backs of countless struggling professional and amateur mathematicians. More than in any other field, we teach the *math* (the end product of the process of mathematics development) and ignore the fascinating *people* and *stories* associated with the development of the field. Mention "math" and "story" in the same sentence and most people shudder in terror, thinking of the dreaded math story problem. ("If John and Carol want to meet in Chicago, and John leaves Denver at 8 AM on a train at 60 mph . . .") Those are *not* stories.

There are fictional stories in our vast body of literature that include math concepts as significant story and plot elements. Two good references to find those stories are *Math Through Children's Literature* by Kathryn L. Braddon, Nancy J. Hall, and Dale Taylor (Teacher Ideas Press) and the *Once Upon a GEMS Guide* by the University of California, Berkeley's Lawrence Hall of Science.

But there is another type of math story. These stories are gripping, fascinating, and illuminate the development, history, and purpose of our modern math tools and concepts. These historical stories concern the real-life drama of the development of math and of the mathematicians who invented it. Precious few of these stories have been written and made available to school-age students and their teachers.

That is why I created this book and these stories. Any topic, math included, becomes more accessible and understandable when we tell the human stories behind the development of the topic. Stories make subjects real and purposeful. They create context and relevance. They provide a foundation from which students can understand and appreciate math, rather than merely memorize a series of rote exercises.

These sixteen stories focus on significant developments in mathematics history. However, all stories are about characters, not concepts, and these stories are no exception. In this case, the characters are amazing, often quirky, but always brilliant and interesting mathematicians. The stories are here because they tell about characters at the moment of significant developments in the math concepts and principals we depend on every day.

While these stories offer a glimpse into the process and development of math, they are also accessible and understandable—even to students who have not yet been exposed to each of the math concepts.

The stories are divided into four groups: the development of our number system, the development of geometry, the development of mathematical concepts and applications, and the development of devices to aid in mathematical computations.

I narrowed the great number of possible stories to these sixteen by using the following four criteria: Significance of the described math development; significance of the central mathematician; diversity of culture, area of math discussed, time period, gender of the central mathematicians; and, finally, whether the development would make a good story.

Some say that math is discovered, that the numbers and concepts were always there, like gravity or air, waiting to be discovered. I disagree. Many of our math processes, concepts, and fields—even parts of our number system, itself—are more accurately the inventions of one or more clever mathematicians. They are things that did not exist until someone invented them. Like any good invention, they seem an obvious and essential part of the system *after* they have been invented. But their development represents an act of imaginative, creative genius, rather than discovery.

Each story is as historically accurate as available research permitted. If I found quotes recorded in diaries or letters, I used them for dialog. Otherwise, I inferred dialog from known personality traits, written accounts, the mathematician's writings and essays, and from known interactions and events. All characters, their physical descriptions, personalities, and roles in the stories, are also as historically accurate as possible. The same is true of the events described.

Yet, I also wanted the stories to be "real" as well as accurate. Each character is a real person with passions, doubts, and fears. To the extent that I could reasonably establish what these emotional states most probably were, I used them to bring the characters to life.

I have written two other story collections which include stories of mathematicians.

I describe brilliant mathematicians in these stories, but they were also lucky. They lived at the right time, in the right place, and had the background to create the opportunity for invention. Mathematics is far from finished. Maybe *you* will be the next person with the opportunity, imagination, insight, and foresight to create the next marvel of math.

I hope you enjoy these stories, and, more importantly, hope they inspire you to learn more about these and other important mathematicians, and about the fascinating history of our mathematics system. Finally, I hope that these stories shed some light on why modern math is the way it is, and provide some insight into the intent and organization of math.

But don't stop there. These are only sixteen of countless fascinating math stories. Research and create your own. There are hundreds of deserving mathematicians and thousands of marvelous stories to write.

I owe a special thanks to two people and one Center for their role in developing this book and these stories. The National Women's History Center in Windsor, California, was an invaluable source of information on the various women mathematicians presented in this book. Dr. Nelson Kellogg at Sonoma State University acted as a trusted advisor throughout the project. He possesses a keen understanding of the history of math and science and of the many individuals that mark its course, and has an irresistible and infectious enthusiasm for each of these mathematicians and their struggles and accomplishments.

Last, Roni Berg has once again acted as the true litmus test for each of these stories. With uncanny accuracy she has helped to reshape each story and ensure each became both exciting and understandable to those with all levels of math literacy. To each of these three I owe an unending debt of gratitude.

Stories
About Numbers

Numbers in the Sand

The Invention of Irrational Numbers by the Pythagoreans circa 520 BC

At a Glance

By the time of the early Greek mathematicians and philosophers, positive whole numbers (integers) and fractions (ratios of two whole numbers) had been created. They called those two groups the "rational numbers."

The idea of having negative numbers had been rejected because, the Greeks concluded, it was impossible to have less than none of something. Therefore, negative numbers had no meaning and could not be included in the system of rational numbers.

The Greeks, under the leadership and teaching of a fiery speaker and mathematician, Pythagoras, gave great importance to the properties of numbers and of groups of numbers. It was a century of worldwide revolution in thought, a time for new ideas. Pythagoras was a contemporary of Buddha, Confucius, and Lao-Tze who revolutionized thought in the eastern world.

The revolutionary ideas that Pythagoras taught centered on the meaning, properties, and all-consuming importance of rational numbers. For Pythagoras, rational numbers held all the secrets of the universe. Until some of his students in 520 BC accidentally upset his delicate apple cart.

Terms to Know

Understanding the following mathematical terms will help you understand and appreciate this story.

1. **Theorem.** A theorem is the statement of a rule or relationship expressed in terms of mathematical symbols and equations. Pythagoras' famous theorem tells us about the relationship of the length of the sides of a certain kind of triangle and is written $a^2 + b^2 = c^2$. Theorems can be proposed at any time, but must be proved in order to be of general use. It is often much easier to see that a relationship *seems* to be true and express it as a theorem, than it is to *prove* that it must *always* be true.

2. **Right Triangle.** A triangle is a shape made of three straight sides. The lines meeting at each corner of a triangle meet at some angle between 0 degrees and 180 degrees. If one of those angles is exactly 90 degrees, the triangle is called a "right triangle" since 90 degrees is called a "right angle."

   Many special and interesting relationships exist for the sides and angles of a right triangle, which have made them a focal point of geometric study since the time of the earliest Greek mathematicians.

3. **Whole Number.** Whole numbers, or integers, are the counting numbers we all first learn as small children (1, 2, 3, 4, 5, etc.). The only other kind of number the early Greeks recognized was a fraction, where a fraction is defined as a ratio of two whole numbers. 1/2 and 3/5 are fractions. So is 275/3489. As long as it can be expressed as the ratio of two whole numbers, the Greeks called it a fraction.

   Whole numbers and fractions made up "rational" numbers. The Greeks thought rational numbers were all the numbers that existed.

4. **Square Root.** The square root of a number is that number which, when multiplied by itself, produces the original number. The square root of 4 is 2. The square root of 9 is 3. The square root of 16 is 4, since 4 x 4 = 16. The mathematical symbol used to mean "the square root of" is "$\sqrt{}$." The mathematical way to write "the square root of 9 is 3," is "$\sqrt{9} = 3$."

   Not all numbers have even square roots as 4, 9, and 16 do. The square root of 2 ($\sqrt{2}$) is approximately 1.414. The $\sqrt{3}$ is approximately 1.732.

5. **The Number Line.** Imagine all numbers being arranged from lowest to highest along one long line. That line and all the numbers on it is called the number line.

   For us, that number line includes positive and negative whole numbers from minus infinity to plus infinity (including zero), positive and negative fractions, and irrational numbers. For Pythagoras and the other early Greeks, that line included only positive whole numbers and positive fractions.

6. **Deductive Reasoning.** Deductive reasoning is the method of thinking through a problem used and taught by Pythagoras. In general, deductive reasoning goes from some general, previously established and proved concept to a particular example, and to a conclusion. For example, first make a general statement: all shapes drawn of three straight sides are triangles. That has been well established by definition. Second, apply a specific example: I have drawn a figure with three, straight sides. Third, draw a conclusion: Therefore, what I have drawn is a triangle.

   As a second example: All boys have two arms. John is a boy. Therefore, John has two arms. The hardest part of deductive reasoning is to be sure that the general concept, or premise, is always true. Do you think the general premise for this second example is always true? or is it *almost* always true? If it isn't always true, it cannot be used as the general premise for deductive reasoning.

Numbers in the Sand

"You tell him."

Philoclease (FIL-o-kleez) scratched through his thick, gray beard and then through his curly white hair before answering. Finally he shook his head. "How can I tell Pythagoras (Peh-THAG-uh-rus) he's wrong? I've been his trusted student for thirty years. *You* tell him."

A soothing breeze blew in from the blue Mediterranean Sea this summer day in the year 517 BC. Its gentle swirl made the Greek colony sea-port of Croton, where Pythagoras' students lived and studied, always feel more bearable than the scorching inland hills of southern Italy.

But then, why did sweat dribble down the faces of Philoclease and Dionesa (Di-o-NEE-sa) as they studied their geometric drawings in the sand? Perhaps it was the terrible heat of their discovery and not the muggy afternoon that flushed their cheeks.

Kneeling beside old Philoclease, thirty-year-old Dionesa stared at their lines drawn in the smooth sand. "Maybe we've made an error. Maybe we haven't used proper deductive reasoning."

But even as she said it, she knew it wasn't true. They *had* used proper deductive reasoning as the great mathematics and philosophy teacher, Pythagoras, had taught them to do. The figures scratched in the sand proved it. Pythagoras, the greatest teacher in the history of mankind, the unchallenged source of all wisdom and learning, the founder and master of the Brotherhood, he who seemed to be the son of the gods themselves, he from whom it seemed all knowledge flowed—*he* was wrong!

His lowly students had just discovered it.

It wasn't some minor detail over which they had just proved Pythagoras' teachings to be in error. That would be bad enough. Philoclease and Dionesa had just proved the very foundation of Pythagoras' teachings to be wrong. It felt as if the ground they stood on had split wide open and they would tumble forever into some endless, black pit.

Philoclease and Dionesa hadn't set out to prove their beloved master wrong. They had wanted to solve a problem and show Pythagoras how much they had learned.

From *Marvels of Math*. © 1998 Kendall Haven. Teacher Ideas Press. (800) 237-6124.

But there sat the proof in the sand before them. Whole numbers (1, 2, 3, 4, etc.) could not describe everything in the world. Pythagoras said that they did. He claimed that everything could be described through either a whole number or through a ratio of whole numbers (a fraction). Philoclease and Dionesa had just proved that the heart of their great master's teachings was wrong.

"*Someone* has to tell Pythagoras," insisted Dionesa. "Isn't the purpose of the Brotherhood of Students to search for truth?"

Born on the Greek Island of Samos in about 572 BC, Pythagoras had traveled to all the great learning centers of the time and had studied extensively before landing in Croton to teach. His first school attempts met with little success. For over a year, he had to pay his students to keep them in school.

But Pythagoras was a fiery speaker, and slowly learned showmanship techniques. He learned to act like an all-knowing authority. He stood tall for his day with a head of short, tightly-curled hair, a trim beard, a stern face, and piercing blue eyes.

Pythagoras would emerge from behind a curtain for public lectures wearing a wreath and bracelets of dazzling gold. He learned to make his deep voice rumble like thunder. His gestures became grand, sharp, and sweeping, and drove away all doubt. His words sounded like commandments from the Greek gods instead of simple mathematical concepts.

Pythagoras would pace across a smooth sand stage as he lectured, drawing geometric shapes, lines, and curves in the raked sand. Important sections were filled in with colored sand by assistants.

Wealthy and aristocratic students soon flocked to Pythagoras' school. But students could not simply buy their way in. New students spent their first few years listening to the master's lectures from behind a thick screen. They could hear, but could not watch the master's teachings.

Only after several years were they admitted into the circle of tiered seats in Pythagoras' small amphitheater, and into the Brotherhood of Pythagoras' students. This Brotherhood had grown to be one of the most powerful and secretive forces in Croton.

Pythagoras taught his students far more than mathematics. He had been schooled in Hindu, Mesopotamian, and Egyptian philosophies, and wove these teachings into the mystic properties of numbers described in his lectures. Pythagoras turned the study of numbers into a religion. (In fact, the Greek word, "mathema" technically referred to any kind of learning, but most commonly meant religious study. Pythagoras was the first to add a suffix and form the word, "mathematike," to mean the study of geometry and numbers.)

Pythagoras taught that simple whole numbers were the key to understanding the universe. The properties of numbers both described the world, and dictated how the world must operate. Pythagoras preached that everything in the universe could be described as either whole numbers or as ratios of whole numbers (one whole number divided by another—what we call fractions). To study the nature and properties of those numbers and fractions, was to learn the true essence of man, nature, and the world.

In Croton everyone believed him, as if his words had been spoken by kings and gods and were the very definition of truth. The motto of the Brotherhood was "Numbers are all."

So Philoclease and Dionesa stared at their drawings in the sand. Who would tell Pythagoras that whole numbers were not all? Who would announce that whole numbers did not describe everything in the world? Who would tell Pythagoras that they had found a number which could not be expressed as a fraction, a ratio of whole numbers? Who would tell Pythagoras that there existed a whole new group of numbers which were not a part of his philosophy?

"I dare not do it," whispered Dionesa, daughter of a wealthy merchant and one of the thirty women in the 250-member Brotherhood. "I have only been a student for five years. How could I tell our master he is wrong? *You* do it!"

Again Philoclease shook his head. "I have been his faithful student for too long to challenge him now. I dare not even *think* of what the Brotherhood would do to anyone who dared to oppose the master. . . . I dare not think what *Pythagoras* would do!" His face slowly brightened. "Let's get Theanna (THEE-an-a) to tell him!"

Theanna was the brilliant daughter of a local Greek magistrate. At first a prized student, she had also been Pythagoras' wife for over ten years.

Summoned by the urgent pleas of a messenger, Theanna raced to the house where Philoclease and Dionesa nervously waited. With her came Hippasus (HIP-a-soos), another long-time Brotherhood member she had met along the way. Consistent with Brotherhood beliefs, Theanna wore simple cotton clothes, even though she could afford the finest silk.

Starting with a smooth sand floor, Philoclease and Dionesa redrew their diagrams, beginning with a right triangle. They rewrote the equations and steps that formed their deductive proof. With a sigh, Philoclease concluded, "We started out to explore the nature of the length of one side of this triangle. In the end what we found is that a certain number, $\sqrt{2}$ (the square root of two), cannot be expressed as a ratio of whole numbers. It is a new and different kind of number completely outside of Pythagoras' philosophy."

"It must not be so!" cried Theanna. "That would destroy the beliefs of the Brotherhood. There must be an error."

Dionesa shook her head. "We have searched for three days. There is no error."

Hippasus, a short man with thick, burly arms and a permanent scowl, demanded, "Tell me again where this number, $\sqrt{2}$, came from. Why were you studying it at all?"

Dionesa answered, "We drew a right triangle as Pythagoras has taught us. We made the length of the two sides both equal to one unit in length."

Theanna and Hippasus nodded. They had each drawn right triangles many times.

Dionesa continued. "Using Pythagoras' great theorem on right triangles, we learned that the length of the third side of the triangle, called the hypotenuse, must have a length equal to $\sqrt{2}$."

Again Theanna and Hippasus nodded. All Brotherhood members had memorized Pythagoras' theorem on right triangles.

Dionesa paused to sadly shrug and sigh. "We eagerly set out to investigate the properties of $\sqrt{2}$, but as you can see, what we found is that it is impossible to express $\sqrt{2}$ as a ratio of whole numbers. Pythagoras is wrong."

The words swept over Theanna like a hurricane, leaving her dazed and speechless.

"Will you tell him?" asked Philoclease.

Theanna continued to stare at the sand drawings. Finally, she shook her head. "He is my husband. I cannot destroy all his teachings. I cannot destroy his life."

"I will," said Hippasus. "The Brotherhood stands for the search for truth. If this proof is wrong, let Pythagoras show us where. If not . . ."

Late that afternoon a lecture was scheduled. The amphitheater filled with Brotherhood members. The stage sand was brushed smooth by assistants. A gong sounded. The crowd quieted. Pythagoras swept aside a curtain and marched to center stage wearing gleaming white robes, a golden wreath around his head.

"Whole numbers and ratios of whole numbers (fractions) we call 'rational' numbers," he began. "These rational numbers hold all the secrets of the universe."

Philoclease and Dionesa sat nervously wringing their hands in the second row. Theanna paced at one side of the tiered amphitheater seats.

"We have already learned much about the nature and properties of different rational numbers and groups of rational numbers. As we learn ever more, I believe we will come to fully understand the essence of man and nature."

Hippasus scowled, arms folded across his chest, on the far side of the curved bleachers.

"I have already discussed the groups of numbers we call amicable, or friendly numbers, the group of perfect numbers, of prime numbers, of even and odd numbers, and of figurative numbers. The unique properties of each of these groups are the keys to understanding life itself. Rational numbers are all that there is."

Hippasus sprang to his feet. "That is not true, Pythagoras. There are more numbers than those."

The crowd of students glared in awe and anger at Hippasus. None dared move. Many hardly dare breathe. Time, itself, seemed to stand still.

No one had ever dared to challenge Pythagoras before. No one had ever made so bold a claim. Pythagoras strode across the stage, his sandaled footprints grinding into sand intended for his drawings. His jaw clenched in anger, he hissed, "Explain yourself, Hippasus. *Prove* yourself."

The first angry mutters to "get him for doubting the master" rumbled through the crowd as Hippasus climbed to the stage. Some started for the stairs to drag Hippasus from the amphitheater.

Pythagoras stopped them with a single raised hand. "Let the truth or falsehood of his mathematike determine Hippasus' fate."

Hippasus used a sharpened stick to draw a right triangle. He labeled the two perpendicular sides each with a length of 1. "Now tell us, Pythagoras, what must be the length of the third side, the hypotenuse?"

Without a moment's hesitation Pythagoras answered, "It must be the $\sqrt{2}$."

"Quite correct," nodded Hippasus. "An interesting number the $\sqrt{2}$." He paused and glanced at Pythagoras. "You admit, don't you, that $\sqrt{2}$ must be a number?"

Pythagoras frowned and nodded.

"Two of my fellow Brotherhood members wanted to see what fraction, or ratio of whole numbers, equaled $\sqrt{2}$. Here is what they found."

Line by line, Hippasus carefully repeated the proof that $\sqrt{2}$ could not be represented by *any* ratio of whole numbers, as Philoclease and Dionesa had shown him. He used half the stage, writing each detail for the master.

As he finished Hippasus flung down the stick and folded his beefy arms. "Well, Pythagoras, is this proof wrong, or do you admit there are things in this world which cannot be described by your rational numbers?"

Many began to boo. A surge of outraged students swept toward the stage. Several threw rocks at Hippasus. Again Pythagoras silenced the mob with a single raised hand.

For a very long time he stood motionless, studying what Hippasus had written, his chin cupped in one hand. Every student froze, silently waiting for their master to react, for him to tell them how to react.

Pythagoras seemed to have aged and shrunk when he finally spoke, his voice drained of thunder. "Hippasus' proof is correct. There *are* numbers which are not within our system of rational numbers." He paused, gazing at his students. "This is the gravest matter ever brought to our attention. Our every belief, our very philosophy has just been challenged. Our power and position could easily crumble. Not one word of this may ever be spoken outside this Brotherhood—not ever!"

Without another word Pythagoras stormed back behind the stage curtain. The stunned students of the Brotherhood were left adrift to manage the shock on their own. Their cozy world of faith had been shattered.

Within a month Hippasus was dead. Officially he died in a boating accident. Some claimed he was murdered for mentioning his "irrational" numbers outside of the Brotherhood. Some simply said it wasn't wise to challenge the master.

Numbers could no longer be trusted to hold all the secrets of the universe. They did not all behave as they were supposed to. For two thousand years this one discovery, this one moment, changed the course of mathematical study. The focus shifted toward geometry and away from direct number manipulation and calculation.

What the Brotherhood called a disaster, we now call the invention of irrational numbers. These numbers (π, $\sqrt{2}$, $\sqrt{3}$, etc.) are an essential and very real part of the continuous number line. We call this line the "real" numbers and know that real numbers include both rational and irrational numbers. But learning and understanding the meaning of all real numbers is another story.

Follow-on Questions and Activities to Explore

1. Have you ever heard of Pythagoras' great theorem on right triangles, the Pythagorean Theorem? Can you find it in the library? How might it be very useful to you?

    Answer: The Pythagorean Theorem states that the sum of squares of the lengths of the two sides of a right triangle which are adjacent to (next to) the right angle, equals the square of the length of the third side, called the hypotenuse. In mathematical language this is written as, $a^2 + b^2 = c^2$.

    You will use this theorem in math, engineering, and science to solve problems involving right triangles, and you might use it sometime to make square corners on a building or box you build.

2. Pythagoras found a few right triangles whose sides were all whole number lengths. The most famous of these is called a 3-4-5 right triangle. If one of the two sides adjacent to the right angle is 3 units long, and the other is 4 units long, then the third side, the hypotenuse, will be exactly 5 units long. Pythagoras' theorem is written, $a^2 + b^2 = c^2$. Substituting the values for a 3-4-5 right triangle, we have $3^2 + 4^2 = 5^2$, which is true since $9 + 16 = 25$.

    You can use this information to create a perfect right angle. Draw a line, mark a dot at one end, and mark a second dot four inches down the line from the first dot. From this second dot use a compass to draw a five inch arc. From the first dot at the end of the line draw a three inch arc. From the point where the two arcs cross, draw a line to your first dot. You have now drawn a perfect right angle. Check it with a protractor.

    As a class, try it again using wood (1-by-4's or 2-by-4's work best) and measuring lengths of 3 feet, 4 feet, and 5 feet. Mark a point 3 feet down one board, and a point 4 feet down a second. Rotate the boards until the dots are 5 feet apart. See if the right angle you construct is as good as any of the corners on your school building.

    Answer: Compare your answer with those of other students and discuss it as a class.

Something from Nothing

The Invention of Zero as a Number
by al-Khwarizmi in AD 800

At a Glance

No one had yet thought of having a number for zero. Not the Greeks, not Aristotle, not Euclid, not Archimedes, not Pythagoras, not the Romans, not the Hebrews. They all studied math and numbers, but didn't use them to solve practical day-to-day problems.

The Greeks and Romans both refused to believe that negative numbers could exist. They reasoned that it was impossible to have less than none of something. So they were never forced to realize that they also needed a number for zero.

Hindu mathematicians in southern India first created zero, but did not recognize it as a number. They used zero only as a placeholder when no number existed. Add 4 + 6. You get 10, 1 in the tens column and none in the ones column. The Hindus realized that they needed a way to indicate that there was no number in units position. They called it "*sifr*," their word for an empty place.

For 400 years that was the only use for zero. No one added, subtracted, multiplied, or divided it. No one thought of whether it should be odd or even. It was only used to hold an empty place for a missing number. So, 2003 could be written differently than 2030 or 23.

Before AD 800 the Hindu number system migrated west into the Arab world. There a brilliant mathematician, al-Khwarizmi, invented zero as a number. He realized that it *had* to be a number in order for the emerging system of algebraic equations to work. Algebra, another word first used by al-Khwarizmi, comes from Arabic, al-jabra, and means the reduction, or the solution.

Interestingly, the Mayan culture in South America developed the concept of a number zero about the same time that the Arabs did. But Mayan math died with Mayan culture, while the Arabic system spread across Europe.

This is the story of the man and the moment when zero became a number and took its rightful place on the number line.

Terms to Know

Understanding the following mathematical terms will help you understand and appreciate this story.

1. **Arithmetic.** Arithmetic is the basic mathematics we all do every day. Arithmetic refers to the use of the four basic operations (addition, subtraction, division, and multiplication) to manipulate numbers. There are no equations or unknown quantities in arithmetic problems. $4 + 8 = 12$ is an example of an arithmetic problem.

2. **Algebra.** Algebra is the branch of mathematics which uses letters or symbols to represent unknown quantities and organizes problems into the form of equations. An equation is a statement of equality. One quantity or group of terms is stated to be equal to some other quantity or group of terms, and that equality is used to solve for the unknown value.

    Algebra uses the same four operations that are used in arithmetic plus squares, square roots (more generally, all exponential powers), and the six periodic functions to solve problems. The difference is how the problem is organized and presented. Algebra allows us to solve much more complex problems than arithmetic. $x = 4 + 8$ is an example of a simple algebra problem.

3. **Powers.** The use of power notation (a^2, a^3, etc.) is short hand for repetitive multiplication. a^2 tells you to multiply two of whatever a represents together (a x a). The "2" is called an exponent. a^3 tells you to multiply three of whatever a represents together (a x a x a). a^4 tells you to multiply four a's together (a x a x a x a). And so forth. You do not need to always raise some quantity to a whole number power. You could write $a^{3.2}$ meaning (a x a x a x a/5). Archimedes was the first to use exponential notation to indicate raising a number to some power. $x^2 = 16$ is a simple algebraic problem using powers.

Something from Nothing

In the center of the oasis city of Baghdad (in what is now Iraq), the great marketplace could be heard and smelled long before it was seen—shouting vendors, haggling customers, bawling camels, the wafting odor of cinnamon and saffron.

Outside the marketplace, the swaying palm trees of Baghdad stretched toward the sky, and the Tigris River flowed wide and blue. Beyond, there was only rolling sand, blazing sun, and dry desert winds, which made every trip seem far too long and weary.

The harshness of the outside world was shed like a winter coat once a traveler stepped into the labyrinth of alleyways, each shaded by billowing cloth screens, and great open squares that made up the sprawling Baghdad marketplace. Silk weavers, book sellers, money changers, herb sellers, shops and carts with spices, perfumes, and foods of all description crammed in next to each other, overloading the senses. Shops and houses of mud bricks formed the walls. Veiled women clustered to gossip in the shade outside dim shops and cubicles. Fortunes rose and fell. Life was made possible.

It was about AD 800. Though the seasons change little in the desert, this was late spring with sweet, juicy dates just ripening on palm trees.

The thick-walled, pleasantly-cool palace of the Caliph, or ruler, rose from a small hill beside the marketplace. On this spring day, a great debate raged in a shaded courtyard of that palace. One of the debaters was Muhammed ibn Musa, known as al-Khwarizmi, forty, just beginning to sprout shocks of gray in his beard and hair. Al-Khwarizmi was the most famous mathematician in the Arab world, the first to be called a *great* mathematician since Aryabhatta three centuries before.

The second man in this debate was the Caliph, Al-Mamum, himself, ruler of Baghdad and all the desert as far as one could ride in a week in any direction. Two servants standing behind his jeweled chair continually, gently fanned the Caliph with wide palm fronds. Twenty years before, Al-Mamum renamed his palace the "House of Wisdom." Ever since, the palace had drawn scholars from every corner of the Arab world like a powerful magnet.

From *Marvels of Math.* © 1998 Kendall Haven. Teacher Ideas Press. (800) 237-6124.

The third man was the palace mathematician, Ahmahd ibn Aziz. Ahmahd always left the impression of looking like a weasel, with quick, jerky movements, long nose, and hungry, beady eyes.

The debate among these three men was about *sifr*, or "the empty place," what we call "zero."

The Caliph was talking, his finger wagging accusingly at al-Khwarizmi. "When you first brought these Hindu numbers to me fifteen years ago and showed us their superiority, we embraced them gladly, and so has all the Arab world. *But*, at that time you clearly stated that *sifr* was merely a placeholder to keep the real numbers in the correct positions when one place was empty and had no number value."

Ahmahd nodded in agreement, his head bobbing like a ferret.

"You are exactly correct, my Caliph," answered al-Khwarizmi. "But on further study, I now conclude that *sifr* is, and must be more than a mere placeholder."

"More?" repeated the Caliph.

"What *more*?" insisted Ahmahd.

"*Sifr*, itself, is a number. It *must be* a number in order for all other numbers, for all arithmetic, and for all algebra to work."

"But *sifr isn't* a number," insisted Ahmahd. "It is a position holder for places which have no number. *Sifr* does not act like a number."

Thoughtfully stroking his trim, pointed beard, the Caliph said, "Ahmahd is right. *Sifr* is different from numbers. How can it now become one of them?"

"We must *make sifr* act like a number," concluded al-Khwarizmi. "If we three cannot do that, mathematics can never advance for the glory of Allah!"

"*How*? How do we make nothing into a something?" asked Ahmahd.

"*Why*? Why can't our math advance without *sifr* being a number?" demanded the Caliph.

"*Your* question, Ahmahd, is simple," answered al-Khwarizmi. "If we make *sifr* do all the things the other numbers do, then it *is* a number. Your question, my Caliph is more difficult to see."

From *Marvels of Math*. © 1998 Kendall Haven. Teacher Ideas Press. (800) 237-6124.

Al-Khwarizmi began to pace as he talked, nibbling on one of the early dates in a large bowl beside the Caliph. "To count, we need no *sifr*. Greeks and Romans proved that. To add and multiply we need only the placeholder of the Hindus. But when we subtract or divide, that is a different story. When you subtract 8 from 8 what do you get?"

"Nothing," answered Ahmahd.

"No. You get *sifr*. 0! Because when you then add 7 back in to this subtraction what do you get?"

"Seven," said the Caliph.

"Exactly, my lord!" answered al-Khwarizmi. "But you could not do that if 0 were not a number, because you cannot add a number to anything other than another number. If 8-8 is not a number, then you can never add 7 back to that sum. The 0 must be a number or subtraction becomes impossible."

Ahmahd's eyes darted back and forth like a trapped animal. He nervously licked his lips.

The Caliph closed his eyes and rocked back and forth before answering. "I agree with your point, my learned friend. They underestimate your powers by calling you great. *But*, all numbers are either positive or negative, are they not? *Sifr* is neither. So how can it be a number?"

"Again you are correct, my lord. *Sifr* is the one number that is neither positive nor negative. It is neither odd nor even. It balances at the mid-point between those two great sets of numbers. It lies at the origin of the number lines, the origin point of every graph of numbers and equations. Only a number at this origin point can complete positive and negative numbers, joining them into a single endless line of numbers."

Ahmahd scratched figures and numbers in the dirt as he spoke. "What you say is only *partly* true. I admit *sifr* acts like a number for counting since it answers the basic question of all numbers, 'How many are there?' when there are none present. I admit you make a strong case that 0 acts like a number for addition and subtraction. *But* a number must also multiply and divide." Ahmahd flipped down his stick and smugly crossed his arms. "Surely you must admit *sifr* can not do those things."

The Caliph thoughtfully raised his eyebrows and turned back to al-Khwarizmi for his answer.

"Division, especially, is what I have spent much time studying. But I will start with multiplication since it is easier to demonstrate."

Al-Khwarizmi loosened a leather purse tied around his waste and pulled out a fistfull of small coins. "If I give you one coin . . ." He tossed a coin to Ahmahd. "And then agree to multiply that sum by four, how many coins must I give you?"

"Four," answered Ahmahd with a shrug.

"Exactly, my friend. I must give you four piles of *one* coin each. Now if I had given you *two* coins . . ." He tossed another coin to the palace mathematician. "And again agreed to multiply this sum by four, how many coins must I give you?"

"Eight, of course. This is basic arithmetic, al-Khwarizmi. What does this have to do with *sifr*?"

Al-Khwarizmi held up one hand for quiet. "Again you are correct. I must give you four piles of *two* coins each."

Al-Khwarizmi reached across and snatched the two coins back from Ahmahd. "And if I give you *sifr* coins and agree to multiply this sum by four, how many must I give you?"

Ahmahd's eyes darted back and forth. He licked his lips. "You can't multiply by *sifr*. It is impossible."

"Wrong, my friend. Exactly as before I must give you four piles, but this time of *no* coins each."

The Caliph leaned forward, eyebrows furrowed in thought. "So you are saying that when 0 is multiplied by any number the answer is always 0. But no other number produces the same answer for all multiplications."

"Exactly my lord. *Sifr* is the most amazing, mysterious, and unique of all numbers. Let us not shun and fear it, but embrace this amazing number as the key to all higher mathematics."

"What of 0 x 0?" sneered Ahmahd.

With a casual shrug al-Khwarizmi answered, "No piles of no coins each is still *sifr*."

"Fascinating," murmured the Caliph. "And what of division?"

From *Marvels of Math*. © 1998 Kendall Haven. Teacher Ideas Press. (800) 237-6124.

Al-Khwarizmi nodded in acknowledgment of this hardest of all questions. "Division by *sifr* is difficult to explain. If I divide 100 coins into 100 piles, each pile has 1 coin. If I divide the coins into 10 piles, each pile has 10 coins. Fewer piles, more coins in each."

He glanced at the Caliph and Ahmahd to be sure they followed his reasoning. "As I reduce the number of piles, each pile gains more coins. As I make the *divisor* smaller and smaller, the *answer* to the division problem grows larger and larger. When I reduce the divisor to one, the answer increases to 100. If I further reduce the divisor from one to *sifr*, the answer must grow larger."

"But larger to *what?*" demanded the Caliph, leaning so far forward, the two servants could barely stretch far enough to fan cool air over his back.

"First, my lord, I considered fractions. We know that it is possible to divide by fractions. Dividing 100 coins by 1/2 is the same as multiplying them by 2. The answer is 200 coins. If I divide by 1/10, the answer is 1000. If I divide by 1/1000, the answer is 100,000. But *sifr* is still smaller. Smaller than 1/1000, smaller than 1/1,000,000. So when dividing by *sifr*, the answer must be very large."

"How large?!" demanded the Caliph.

"I pondered long on this question, my Caliph. Finally I used graph paper to determine the answer. As the number of piles grows so small as to disappear into nothing, or 0, the number of coins in each pile must grow so large as to increase to infinity. Since we know infinity is not a number, but a description for a place beyond numbers, the answer is that any number divided by *sifr* is indefinite."

"Ha!" sneered a suddenly triumphant Ahmahd. "You admit it won't work."

"But that still makes *sifr* a number because I can *do* the division, even though I don't get one of the specific numbers we know as an answer. If *sifr* weren't a number I couldn't do the division at all."

Ahmahd's face drooped into a disappointed sulk.

The Caliph thoughtfully rubbed his beard as he scowled.

From *Marvels of Math*. © 1998 Kendall Haven. Teacher Ideas Press. (800) 237-6124.

A messenger arrived, bowed, and whispered in the Caliph's ear.

Al-Mamum nodded, rose, and turned sternly to al-Khwarizmi. "I must leave. You argue well for your new number. When you brought me the Hindu number system I could see its value, a value that has proven itself to be many times greater than I foresaw. I can *begin* to see the benefit to our algebra and arithmetic of having a regular number for 0. But I'm not yet convinced *sifr can* be a number. We will talk more tomorrow."

Al-Khwarizmi and Ahmahd both bowed low as the Caliph and his servants swept past, leaving the courtyard in stony silence, broken only by the whisper of a desert wind, the rustle of fronds in the tall date palms, and the distant calls of the marketplace.

∽ ∽ ∽

"Answer two questions and I will be convinced that you have created a new number for the world to use."

It was late the next afternoon. The same trio had gathered in the Caliph's council room. The Caliph perched on a cushioned throne. The two mathematicians squatted at his feet.

"First, you say any number divided by 0 is infinitely large and thus undefined. Is this true for *sifr*, itself? Can *sifr* be divided by itself, and what is the answer if it is?"

Ahmahd chuckled at the cruel difficulty of the question.

Al-Khwarizmi answered without a moment's hesitation. "The division you mention is a special case within the special case for division by 0. Nothing cannot be divided into groups at all, and especially not into no groups. That unique division problem must be labeled 'undefined.' "

Ahmahd quickly pointed out, "Doesn't that mean that *sifr* isn't a real number?"

"It means only that our ignorance of mathematics prevents us from understanding these special cases of division."

"But *sifr* is still a number?" asked the Caliph.

"Most definitely, my lord."

The Caliph nodded. "I accept. Second, Aristotle created the concept and notation for raising one number to the power of another number. Thus, $4^2 = 16$, or 4 x 4. $4^3 = 64$, or 4 x 4 x 4. What is 4^0, or, more generally, what is any number, x^0?"

"An excellent question, my lord."

"I know. Answer it!"

Al-Khwarizmi bowed. "x^3 is x times x times x (or x^2 times x). x^2 is x times x (or x^1 times x). x^1 equals x. This is basic algebra. . ."

"I see where you are going," interrupted the Caliph. "x^0 would be no x's or 0."

"No, my lord. For x^1 is x^0 times x, just as $x^3 = x^2$ times x. If x^0 were 0, then x^1 would also be 0 (0 times anything is 0). But it is not. x^0 must be *1*."

Ahmahd squealed, "What?!"

The Caliph laughed. "Very good, al-Khwarizmi. You have out-thought me again. Of course, you must be correct. Well done, my friend. You have proved your point. As of this date *sifr is* a number, not just a placeholder. Our number line runs unbroken from minus infinity to plus infinity with your *sifr* holding the sides together in the middle."

This one act of insight and creative genius under a hot Arab sun made possible all of algebra, calculus, trigonometry, and most other branches of math, engineering, and science. Without zero as a real part of the number line, without this most profound mathematical discovery, we would be able to do little more than count, even today.

But the world fought against this grand discovery and resisted its use for another 500 years. Why, of course, is another story.

Follow-on Questions and Activities to Explore

1. Do you think zero is a particularly interesting and unique number? Make a list of all the unique properties of zero, both those mentioned in this story and others you can think of.

   Answer: Zero is unique in the following ways:

   ✧ It is neither odd nor even, neither positive nor negative.

   ✧ It is not a prime number, but is not divisible by any other number.

   ✧ Zero is not factorable.

   ✧ When zero is added to or subtracted from any other number, it leaves that other number unchanged.

   ✧ Multiply zero times any number and the answer is zero. It is the only number for which the answer to all multiplications is the same number.

   ✧ Zero is the only number whose divisions all have no answer because the answer is always infinity, an undefined number.

   ✧ Any number raised to the zero power is one. Numbers raised to any other power always produce different number answers.

2. Do other numbers have unique properties? List any others you think of and those unique properties.

   Answer: One and infinity both have several unique properties. Use the list of properties above to see if you can find the unique properties of these two numbers.

Imagine That...

**The Invention of Imaginary Numbers
by Rafael Bombelli in 1545**

At a Glance

Babylonians in 3000 BC could write and solve complicated mathematical expressions. Each great society thereafter advanced our knowledge of math, leaving a legacy of development and progress. But, as the sixteenth century dawned, one important aspect of western mathematics development had ground to a halt for over a thousand years. Mathematicians seemed to be blocked by a mighty stone wall, a kind of equation that could not be solved.

These pesky equations, which befuddled every noble attempt at a solution, were the ones in which some unknown quantity ("x") was multiplied by itself three times. The term was written x^3 (x cubed). The equations were called cubics. And no one could solve an equation when one of those terms existed in it.

In a practical sense, the great Arabian mathematician, al-Kashi, developed ways to find an *approximate* solution around 600 AD. But no one could actually solve cubics.

It seemed that all mathematical development was bottled up, waiting for that one solution to be found. Hundreds of mathematicians across the western world struggled with the cruel equations for a lifetime, all to no avail.

The greatest concentration of these mathematicians through the fourteenth, fifteenth, and sixteenth centuries was in Italy. As the sixteenth century opened, the wall began to crack. Cubic solutions emerged. But it seemed that many were far more interested in claiming the credit and possessing the glory of the solution, than in understanding the mathematics involved. A drama ensued worthy of any soap opera.

Terms to Know

Understanding the following mathematical terms will help you understand and appreciate this story.

1. **x³ (Cubics).** When some term in an algebraic equation is multiplied times itself three times, it is written "x^3," it is read "x cubed," and it means "x times x times x." Two cubed is written 2^3, is read "two cubed," and it equals 2 x 2 x 2, or 8.

    The "3" is called an exponent. It tells you how many times to multiply the number times itself.

    Cubic equations (equations with an x^3 term in them) are especially hard to solve. This story tells about the first mathematicians to find a way to solve cubics.

2. **Square Root.** The square root of a number is that number which, when multiplied by itself, produces the original number. The square root of 4 is 2. The square root of 9 is 3. The square root of 16 is 4, since 4 x 4 = 16. The mathematical symbol used to say "the square root of" is "$\sqrt{}$." The mathematical way to write "the square root of 9 is 3," is "$\sqrt{9} = 3$."

    Not all numbers have even square roots like 4, 9, and 16. The square root of 2 ($\sqrt{2}$) is approximately 1.414. The $\sqrt{3}$ is approximately 1.732.

3. **Number Line.** Imagine all numbers being arranged from lowest to highest along one long line. That line and all the numbers on it is the number line.

    For us that number line includes positive and negative whole numbers from minus infinity to plus infinity (including zero), positive and negative fractions, and irrational numbers. For Pythagoras and the other early Greeks, that line included only positive whole numbers and positive fractions.

Imagine That . . .

By 1525 Scipione del Ferro was a very old man. He had taught math at the University of Bologna, Italy, all his adult life. He loved and cherished the University and wanted it to be the undisputed center of mathematics development in the world. His greatest pleasure was to totter across campus and soak in the sights and sounds of the plazas, buildings, and bustling students.

Late in the spring term of that year, Scipione called his favorite student, Antonio Fior (FEE-or), into his private study. Antonio was the second son of a powerful family in Bologna. His older brother would inherit the family lands and fortune. Antonio planned to spend his life teaching at the University.

Professor Scipione closed and locked his study door as Antonio entered. From behind a secret panel he removed a metal chest and unlocked it. From inside he handed Antonio eight pieces of paper. "Memorize these."

With a pounding heart, Antonio realized what he held in his hands. "You have solved a cubic equation!"

On the pages in his now-trembling hands, Antonio held the exact solution for *one* cubic equation, written in the form, $x^3 + mx = n$, where m and n are any ordinary numbers.

Antonio sprang to his feet. For a thousand years mathematicians had dreamed of solving some form, any form, of a cubic equation. And his teacher had! "You've done what no one else can do! We must tell this to the world!"

Scipione held out a wrinkled and shaking hand. "No. We will not. This is a solution to only *one* form of a cubic equation. We must secretly discover solutions to them all. Besides, once published, the whole world will have this solution. While it remains unpublished, it belongs to the University of Bologna alone. When I am gone you will continue the work in secret and build the power of this University."

Ten years later, in 1535, an itinerant mathematician, Nicolo of Brescia, announced that he was the first in the world to solve a cubic equation, having solved a cubic in the form, $x^3 + mx^2 = n$.

Most of the world scoffed and ignored him.

From *Marvels of Math.* © 1998 Kendall Haven. Teacher Ideas Press. (800) 237-6124.

Nicolo had raised himself as an Italian rag-a-muffin street urchin. Caught in the midst of a battle between Italian and French soldiers as an eight-year-old boy, Nicolo had his jaw smashed and his chin, mouth, palate, and cheek slashed open by a French sword. He was left on the field for dead.

Nicolo survived. But his jaw and mouth never properly healed. He had great difficulty speaking and was ever after called *Tartaglia*, the stutterer.

Tartaglia (Tar-TAG-lee-a) had only spent three days in school in his life, all his mother could afford. He made good use of those three days, learning half the alphabet and stealing five books to later teach himself how to read.

With floppy, stained cap, curly, grizzled beard, and patchwork clothes, thirty-four-year-old Tartaglia supported himself as an itinerant math tutor.

So when Tartaglia announced that he had solved a cubic and done what the world's great mathematical minds had not been able to do after a millennium of trying, the world brushed him off as a fool.

Except for Antonio Fior.

Antonio was outraged. The credit should be *his*. He had held the secret to solving a cubic for a decade. He could not sit quietly by and let some beggar steal his spotlight.

Assuming Tartaglia's claim was a hoax, Fior challenged him to a public contest to solve cubic equations. Fior planned to use the contest to reveal his own cubic solution to the world. He planned to claim his rightful glory, the fame and praise of his peers, and his spot in history.

Fior and Tartaglia's solutions, of course, were to two slightly different forms of a cubic equation, $x^3 + mx = n$, and $x^3 + mx^2 = n$. There were also many other possible forms of a cubic equation ($x^3 = n$; $x^3 + mx^2 + nx = p$; etc.)

Streetwise Tartaglia realized Fior wouldn't dare make the challenge without having a solution of his own. Tartaglia decided he could only win the contest if he knew *both* solutions. He searched the University of Bologna campus for a needy and dishonest math student, and hired him to steal Fior's solution.

With solutions to *two* forms of the cubic equation in his mind, Tartaglia easily won the contest. Fior was disgraced and fired from the University.

From *Marvels of Math*. © 1998 Kendall Haven. Teacher Ideas Press. (800) 237-6124.

It had been known for some time that any equation with an x^2 term would always have two solutions. That is, there would be two correct answers to the equation. An equation with an x^3 term should have three solutions, and so on.

Fior and Tartaglia found only one or two solutions to each cubic equation they were able to solve in the contest. But no one noticed or cared in all the excitement as the contest ended.

But the story is just beginning.

Another mathematician and teacher, Girolamo Cardano (car-DAH-no), heard of the contest. Especially, he heard that neither Fior nor Tartaglia had published their methods of solving cubics. Cardano saw an opportunity.

Girolamo Cardano was as self-absorbed, wicked, brilliant, scheming, and talented as any mathematician in the history of the western world. He stood tall and thin with large, sad eyes, a bulging forehead, and a long, droopy face with a trim, pointed beard. From the side, his head looked like a crescent moon.

Cardano invited Tartaglia to visit him at the University of Milan, where Cardano was teaching (having been fired from several other universities across Europe). The invitation included an offer of substantial pay to ensure Tartaglia would accept. Over bottles of wine and tankards of ale during the visit, Cardano gleaned the secrets to solving cubics from his unsuspecting guest.

In 1540 Cardano published his great *Ars Magma*, the greatest single work on algebraic methods to date. In it, he presented Tartaglia and Fior's solutions and claimed that they were his own, that he had developed them himself.

Tartaglia was outraged. So was Fior. Both men accused Cardano of stealing, a most serious charge, and tried to sue.

Cardano claimed that he had been the first to develop both solutions and that he had graciously shared one with Scipione del Ferro, and one with Tartaglia. Cardano thus accused both Fior and Tartaglia of plagiarism, or stealing.

Charges, threats, and challenges raged back and forth. Lodovico Ferrari, a brute, thug, and one of Cardano's students, stepped forward to defend his teacher's honor. Fior dropped his claims and fled for fear of being killed by Ferrari.

Tartaglia held his ground. Ferrari left him beaten and badly wounded in a field outside Milan, his jaw once again crushed.

During all the turmoil, another Italian mathematician, Rafael Bombelli, quietly studied everyone's cubic solutions from the sidelines. Bombelli was a rotund, jolly man with a permanent smile plastered under his bushy beard, and a tendency to treat everything with great mouthfuls of laughter.

Bombelli realized that the greatest discovery was not the long-sought solutions to cubics themselves, but rather the very thing everyone had overlooked in their rush to claim the credit. Bombelli realized that solving cubics had uncovered a whole new set of numbers.

Solving cubics always involved taking the square root of a number. If that number happened to be a negative number, -2 for example, Fior, Tartaglia, and Cardano simply ignored the solution. Everyone knew it was impossible to take the square root of a negative number. So solutions which called for it were ignored as impossible solutions.

Everyone knew that there was no number that could be multiplied times itself to produce a negative number. $+1 \times +1 = +1$. $-1 \times -1 = +1$. Every number, when multiplied by itself, produces a positive number—always. So there could be no such thing as the square root of a negative number.

Bombelli realized it would be more correct to say, "Any number *that we know about*, when multiplied by itself, produces a positive number." He realized that there had to be, that there *were*, the correct number of solutions to every cubic equation. It was just that some of these solutions used a new group of numbers, a group that no one had invented.

Bombelli's new group of numbers were the first set of numbers that did not appear on the continuous line of real numbers running from minus infinity to plus infinity. But they were numbers just the same.

Bombelli called his new numbers "imaginary" numbers because they did not appear on the number line. He labeled imaginary numbers with an "*i*" to show that they were part of this new number group. 1 is a positive number;

-1 is a negative number; $1i$ is a positive imaginary number; and $-1i$ is a negative imaginary number.

What is an imaginary number? When two imaginary numbers are multiplied together, they produce a negative number. $3i \times 4i = -12$. The square root of a negative number is an imaginary number. $\sqrt{-1} = 1i$. When a number has both a real number part and an imaginary number part, it is called a "complex" number.

In the end Antonio Fior died alone and unnoticed in his brother's home. Tartaglia returned to his itinerant ways, and died an unknown pauper.

Because of his book and many subsequent articles, Girolamo Cardano has always received the credit for discovering the first solutions to cubics, and is still considered a great mathematician. He was, however, arrested for heresy and spent most of his later years in jail.

Rafael Bombelli lived a happy life and died surrounded by family at the age of 82.

More importantly, Bombelli left behind a whole new class of numbers, a new *kind* of number. Bombelli's imaginary numbers have allowed modern engineers and scientists to complete the complex calculations necessary to successfully design ocean piers capable of withstanding massive storm waves, space shuttles capable of withstanding the stresses of re-entry, and earthquake-resistant skyscrapers. Of course, each of those is another story.

From *Marvels of Math.* © 1998 Kendall Haven. Teacher Ideas Press. (800) 237-6124.

Follow-on Questions and Activities to Explore

1. We all know what positive numbers, negative numbers, and fractions are. We can see them, understand them, and use them. What *is* an imaginary number? Can you see one in real world? Where? What are they used for?

   Answer: Imaginary numbers do not exist in our physical world. They are only an abstract idea. They exist only on paper to aid in the process of solving complex problems. You will never see one. However, you might use one if you advance to college engineering courses.

2. What is a negative imaginary number? What do you think the square root of an imaginary number would be?

   Answer: Imaginary numbers, themselves, are an abstract concept, created only to let us take square roots of negative numbers. No real work has been done on defining the square root of an imaginary number. Certainly it cannot be another imaginary number, since two imaginary numbers, multiplied together, produce a negative number.

   See if you can find any references or information in your local public or university library or on the Internet.

Infinity . . . and Beyond!

The Invention of "Surreal" Numbers by John Conway and Martin Kruskal in 1992

At a Glance

When humans began to count, they created words for each number and also a word for numbers bigger than they could count. It appears that many early tribes had specific numbers for one through nineteen, and, where we would continue with twenty, they went straight to the word for "more than I can count."

Over time, our ability to count ever larger numbers has increased, so that we now have specific names for numbers as high as a one followed by sixty zeros—a number even larger than the national debt. Still there are always numbers beyond our ability to count. Over time the word "infinity" has come into use to describe all such numbers.

For many centuries, infinity has represented an unreachable break-down point for our number system. We intuitively know that if you have infinity of something and add three more to the pile, you have more than you did before. But you still have exactly infinity of them. We don't worry that the logic of our number system breaks down as you approach infinity, because we've never used numbers that get close to infinity.

But with recent improvements in microscopes and telescopes, sub-atomic physicists and astronomers are beginning to bump into the infinitesimally small and the infinitely large. Finally, it is becoming bothersome that our number system doesn't describe the phenomena we call infinity and infinitesimally small (defined as $1 \div \infty$, where ∞ is the mathematical symbol for infinity).

As always seems to happen when a mathematical problem arises, some mathematician rises to the occasion with a mathematical solution. In this case it was two mathematicians at Rutgers University who have galloped to the rescue by inventing "surreal" numbers which let us merrily count to as many infinities as we like.

Terms to Know

Understanding the following mathematical terms will help you understand and appreciate this story.

1. **Ordered Numbers.** Our number system is called "ordered" because it passes two important tests. First, if one number (a) is larger than a second number (b), and if that second number (b) is larger than some third number (c), then the first number (a) *must* be larger than the third (c). Said in mathematical notation, If a>b, and b>c, then a>c.

    Second, if some number (a) is equal to a second number (b), and if that second number is equal to some third number (c), then the first number (a) must be equal to the third (c). Again, in mathematical notation this says, if a = b, and b = c, then a = c.

    These tests seem obvious and trivial because our number system passes both. But imagine what would happen to math problems if our number system didn't pass them.

2. **Infinity.** Infinity is not a number. It is a term to mean "beyond all known numbers," or "bigger than we can count or measure." The mathematical symbol for infinity is "∞." The opposite of infinity is infinitesimal, meaning "so small that we can't measure or count it."

3. **Discontinuity Point.** Any equation with two unknown quantities (usually called "variables," or "unknowns") can be graphed. The equation $x = 2y + 7$ is a simple example. Pick any value for y, and you can calculate a corresponding value for x. Plot each of these pairs of values on a graph, and connect the points with a line. That is the graph of the equation. Each point on that line lies right next to each adjacent point so that the graph forms a smooth, continuous line.

    However, some more complex equations have points where the graph seems to jump. The graph of the equation flows as a normal smooth curve. Then, all of a sudden, it jumps to some other value and continues from there. The point of that jump is called a discontinuity point, because the graph of the equation is not smooth and continuous at that point.

    The problem with discontinuity points is that we can't solve an equation at that point. It seems to have many different solutions, or values, and yet really has none of them. Discontinuity points are a major problem for design engineers because they don't know what will happen at that point.

4. **Equation.** An equation is the general form used to solve algebraic problems. In an equation two mathematical quantities, or terms, are set equal to each other. The equal sign (=) is used to connect the two terms.

    $x = 3a + 2b$ is an equation. It means that the quantity *x* (whatever that is) is exactly equal to three times whatever *a* represents plus two times whatever *b* represents. It is essential to know what is equal to what in solving an algebraic equation.

Infinity . . . and Beyond!

August 1992 sat steamy-hot on Bergen, New Jersey, just north of New York City and across the Hudson River. A thick carpet of shade trees over lawns and sidewalks couldn't hold back the heat from soaking deep into every living thing in town.

Two neighbor children sprawled in the deep shade of a walnut tree. Nine-year-old Yvonne Riggs had shoulder-length blond hair that swung back and forth like a bead curtain every time she turned her head. She lived in the two-story, wood-frame house on the left.

Eight-year-old George Kruskal was thin and wiry, and had freckles thick as stars on a clear night sky. They seemed to form all the major constellations across his cheeks and nose. He lived in the one-story brick house on the right.

"Wish I had a lemonade," said Yvonne, lazily fanning her face with one hand.

"Wish I had *two* lemonades," grumbled George.

"If you get two, I get three."

Though friends, George and Yvonne glared at each other like stalking predators, like gladiators in the arena.

"I get ten lemonades!"

"Oh, yeah?"

"Yeah!"

They began to circle each other like boxers looking for an opening to attack.

"Then I get one hundred."

"Do not."

"Do too!"

"Then I get a million!"

"Oh yeah? I get a billion-zillion-trillion!"

They closed in, nose to nose as they yelled.

From *Marvels of Math*. © 1998 Kendall Haven. Teacher Ideas Press. (800) 237-6124.

"Do not!"

"Do so!"

"I get infinity," announced George.

"There is no such number."

"Is too. It's bigger than you'll ever count. And *that's* how many I get!"

Yvonne hesitated, clenching her fists. "Then I get infinity plus one."

"There is no such number, Yvonne. Infinity is as big as numbers go."

"Is not. How ever many *you* get, I get one more."

Now it was George's turn to hesitate. Was infinity plus one legal? Could she do that?

George's great-uncle, Rutgers University math professor Martin Kruskal, pulled into the driveway and climbed out of his black, aging Buick.

George dashed to the car. Yvonne followed, fearing she was now out-numbered, two to one, in the lemonade argument.

"Tell her, Uncle Martin! It's not legal to have infinity plus one."

"Is, too!" interrupted Yvonne. "If you can have infinity, I can have one more."

Sixty-eight-year-old Martin glanced from child to child pondering the correct answer, "I suppose you *could* have infinity plus one . . ."

Yvonne sneered "Ha!" in triumph. George frowned in dismay.

"*But*," continued Martin. "Infinity plus one is the same as infinity."

"That can't be! It's one more," cried Yvonne.

"Then I have ten infinity plus *two*." Now George crossed his arms and sneered.

"But that's also the same as infinity," explained Uncle Martin.

"That's dumb," said Yvonne. "Everybody knows ten times something is more than the something."

"No. They're both just infinity."

Yvonne laughed. "You mean if I take one away from infinity, I still have infinity?" Now she laughed harder, crueler, and *at* George. "I thought you said he knew math. Everyone knows that's not how numbers work."

"Tell the *real* truth Uncle Martin," pleaded George. "Please!"

"That *is* the truth. Infinity plus anything is still infinity. Two times infinity is infinity. You see, infinity isn't a normal number. It means, 'beyond numbers'."

Yvonne shook her head and whispered to George, "He doesn't know."

Sadly George nodded in agreement. His eyes dropped in disappointment. The children drifted toward Yvonne's yard to play.

The next morning Martin Kruskal sat in the Rutgers math department conference room. His meeting with George and Yvonne still bothered him. Even eight-year-old children knew something was wrong with infinity. Yvonne had been right. It didn't make sense. It didn't act like part of the number system.

Martin leaned back in his hard-back metal chair, gazing off into distant space through deep-set dark eyes, fingers drumming on the Formica table. The one window air conditioner hummed loudly, trying to keep ahead of the heat.

Visiting English mathematician, fifty-six-year-old John Conway, and two students wandered in still discussing a math problem from last Friday's class.

"We have a problem, John," announced Martin, without formal greeting as he allowed the front legs of his chair to crash back to the floor.

"And good morning to you, too, Martin," answered John Conway, his pale, blue eyes seeming to sparkle with laughter as they so often did. "What's our big problem for this hot Monday morning?"

"Infinity. We keep bumping into infinity, and it refuses to act like an *ordered* number. Our whole number system collapses as it approaches the infinite. And we can't ignore it any longer."

Having an ordered number system is critical. Being "ordered" means that if one number, say 5, is larger than a second number, say 3, and that if that second number is bigger than some third number, say 1, then the first number *must* be larger than the third. It also means that if two quantities, a and b, are equal (a = b), and if one of those quantities, a, is equal to some third quantity, c, (a = c), then b *must* also equal c (b = c).

Our number system is ordered—until you get near infinity.

John Conway turned one of the straight-back chairs so he could sit and lean across the chair back. "We have a bigger problem than just that, Martin. The number system still has gaps."

Martin nodded. Both students, thoroughly confused, sank into chairs to listen. "What gaps?" whispered one. The other shrugged.

John explained. "Number systems have always had gaps. When they become a problem, new number systems are discovered or invented to fill the gaps."

Both students still looked confused, so John continued. "First there were only integers—1, 2, 3, 4, etc.—because people only needed to count. But there was nothing between the integer numbers. Four and five existed, but not four-and-a-half. When humans created division, the gaps were a big problem. So fractions were invented, the numbers between whole integers. But there were still gaps between some fractions, so we created irrational numbers, and then imaginary numbers. Now we have bothersome gaps again."

"What gaps?" asked one student.

"There is a gap between zero and the smallest real number fraction. As we develop the ability to measure nearly infinitesimally small quantities—say measurements of some sub-atomic particle activity—that gap is a problem. We can't measure or describe it. Another occurs as you approach infinity. Astronomers measuring the size of the universe are bumping up against that one. Other gaps occur in the solutions to complex equations at what are called discontinuity points. We can't describe or measure the equation there. It creates terrible problems for design engineers."

Martin Kruskal nodded. "Those gaps could destroy the number system."

Both students laughed. Surely this was a joke. "The number system works just fine," said one.

Conway and Kruskal arched their eyebrows. "That's only because you ignore the problems by pretending that some kinds of functions and equations can't be solved. If you tried to solve those equations you'd bump into big problems. And it's getting harder to pretend."

"But . . . but problems *can't* be solved at a discontinuity point," stammered one student.

"We *should* be able to solve them," said Martin Kruskal.

"How?"

"By creating a new, better number system," answered Conway.

Again both students laughed and shook their heads. "Very funny professor." This had to be a practical joke.

"I'm serious," snapped Conway.

Again Kruskal gazed off into the distance, as if staring at infinity, itself. "A new number system. . . . That might work." Now he cupped his hands under his chin and glanced at Conway. "Cantor?"

John Conway nodded. "It seems the obvious starting point."

"What's Cantor?" asked one of the students.

"Not 'what.' Who."

"Then, *who* is Cantor?"

"Shame on you," scolded Kruskal. "You haven't kept up with your history of math readings. Georg Cantor was a nineteenth-century German mathematician. He struggled to tame the unorderliness of infinity. He might have done it, too—except for one thing. He needed to know how big infinity was. Even though he tried up to the day he died, he couldn't figure it out."

The students glanced at each other. This still sounded more like a joke than the truth. "No one knows how big infinity is."

Martin broke into a mischievous smile and gestured to John Conway like a master of ceremonies bringing on the main act. "Take it away, John."

"We may have solved that problem," said John. "We're still testing and experimenting. But we've got something interesting."

He rose and walked to the conference room blackboard. He wrote one Greek letter on the board, "Ω" and tapped it with his chalk. "Omega."

Both students shrugged. "What's omega?"

"That's our new number to describe how big infinity is. If you count for ever, you'll get to infinity, and you will have counted omega times."

The students glanced at each other for support. "But you still don't know how big omega is."

"But it *is* a real, ordered number," answered John. "Now infinity + 1, which we can't define, is $\Omega+1$, which is just an ordinary large number. Now $\Omega+2 > \Omega+1 > \Omega > \Omega-1$. Instantly, infinity is ordered! It gives us a whole new set of working numbers beyond infinity. The number system works again."

Both students struggled to understand. "But . . . but . . . you still don't know how big Ω is. Isn't that cheating?"

"Certainly not," interrupted Martin Kruskal. "Just because *we* don't know exactly how big Ω is, doesn't mean it doesn't exist as a number."

John continued. "And these surreal numbers . . ."

"*What* kind of numbers?" stammered one of the students.

John chuckled. "Martin created the name. We call these new numbers 'surreal' numbers. Do you see how they can fill in the gaps in our current number system?"

Both students slowly shook their heads.

"Think!" snapped Martin. "We just showed you how they fill in gaps near, at, and above infinity. How big are the gaps around zero?"

"Infinitesimally small?" offered one student.

"Define 'infinitesimal,' " said Martin.

One of the students answered, "It's one divided by infinity, or $1 \div \Omega$."

"Exactly," continued Martin. "And if that still leaves a gap use $1 \div 2\Omega$, or $1 \div (\Omega x \Omega)$. There is no point in those gaps we now can't define. The gaps are filled."

A bell rang.

Both students gratefully rose to leave, their minds churning with these new concepts. "Beyond infinity. . . . That's going to take some getting used to," muttered one.

From *Marvels of Math.* © 1998 Kendall Haven. Teacher Ideas Press. (800) 237-6124.

The other glanced over her shoulder to make sure neither John nor Martin could hear. "I still think it's a joke."

But Conway and Kurskal's surreal numbers are a very real, and very new part of our ever-growing number system. They let the infinitely large and the infinitely small act like ordinary numbers. Scientists are just beginning to explore the potential uses of surreal numbers in astronomy, sub-atomic physics, and complex engineering. But how surreal numbers will change the world of the next century is another story.

Follow-on Questions and Activities to Explore

1. Make a list of the biggest and smallest numbers you have ever seen, of the biggest and smallest numbers you know. Who do you think uses bigger numbers and why?

    Answer: Compare your answer with other students and discuss as a class.

2. Is anything infinitely large? Infinitesimally small? If so, what? What are the biggest and smallest things you have ever seen or heard of? How close do they come to being either infinitely large or infinitesimally small? How big would a pile of infinite pennies be?

    Answer: Compare your answer with other students and discuss as a class.

Stories
About Geometry

Elementary
Elements

*The Invention of Euclidean Geometry
by Euclid in 295 BC*

At a Glance

Schooling in early civilizations was a luxury reserved for the rich and well-connected. Schools were few and far between and were built around the philosophy and teachings of each individual school creator and master. Teachers needed no special training or certification. Curricula varied radically from school to school. There were no textbooks, or universally agreed upon set of concepts or methodology to teach.

Into that chaotic world (circa 310 BC) blossomed the Alexandria Museum and Library in Egypt. The Library quickly became the greatest repository of literature, philosophy, art, astronomy, geometry, history, and mathematics in the known world. The Museum, what we would call a university, was humankind's first attempt to gather experts in every field of study together to form the nucleus of a comprehensive teaching faculty. Teachers were sought across Africa, the Mediterranean, Greece, the Middle East, and India. Students and scholars flocked to the Museum to debate and exchange ideas, and to the Library to study.

A Greek named Euclid was hired by King Ptolemy to head the Museum's mathematics department. Euclid proved to be a knowledgeable mathematician and an exceptional teacher. He did not develop new math concepts as had Hippocrates, Theudius, Eudoxius, Aristeus, and Plato before him. What Euclid did was write the world's first comprehensive, logically organized, understandable mathematics textbook. He called it *The Elements*.

The Elements made mathematics accessible to anyone who could read. That one book shaped human thinking on mathematics for two thousand years and defined the way math is still taught. Needless to say, it made Euclid a famous and very popular teacher, whether he liked it or not.

Terms to Know

Understanding the following mathematical terms will help you understand and appreciate this story.

1. **Proof.** To prove something is to demonstrate that it *must* be true. The one field in mathematics that uses proofs is geometry. Beginning with, and building from known truths and factual relationships, a proof tries to logically show that some new concept or theorem must also always be true.

2. **Theorem.** A theorem is the statement of a rule or relationship expressed in terms of mathematical symbols and equations. Pythagoras' famous theorem tells us about the relationship of the length of the sides of a certain kind of triangle and is written $a^2 + b^2 = c^2$.

   Theorems can be proposed at any time, but must be proved to be of general use. It is often much easier to see that a relationship *seems* to be true and express it as a theorem, than it is to *prove* that it must *always* be true.

3. **Axiom.** An axiom is a theorem that is so self-evident that it can be accepted without proof. An example is that a straight line may be drawn which will connect any two points (one of Euclid's axioms). We can accept that as always being true without exhaustive proof. Axioms are the basic building blocks of all subsequent proofs and theorems.

4. **Assumption.** A mathematical assumption is really a guess. Mathematicians make assumptions stating what they think is true, and then try to prove or disprove it.

5. **Concept.** A concept is a general idea. Usually concepts are built on a series of specific examples and then must be proved. For example, you could walk into a fourth-grade classroom and ask six students how old they were. If all six said they were ten years old, you could conclude, as a concept, that all fourth graders are ten. Then you'd have to prove it. In so doing, you might have to amend your concept to say that *almost* all fourth graders are either nine or ten years old.

Elementary Elements

Dry winds swirled off the Egyptian desert onto the fertile Nile River Valley, as hot and searing as a baker's oven. Somehow those winds always felt milder and smelled sweeter when they reached the busy seaport of Alexandria, even though a fierce Mediterranean sun lashed down its heat. Workers in cotton tunics busily loaded and unloaded rows of ships with oars stowed and sails furled. The towering lighthouse of Alexandria silently stood watch over the harbor and magnificent city beyond.

It was April of 295 BC. The port of Alexandria swarmed with bustling activity. Urns, kegs, barrels, bails, and mounds of food, cloth, wine and a thousand other goods were stacked in long rows.

Two blocks back from the docks stood the columned palace of King Ptolemy (TOL-eh-mee), built in classic Greek style. The building rose so wondrous and proud it took your breath away. Beside this palace stood Ptolemy's greatest prize, the Museum and Library of Alexandria, the greatest center of teaching and research in the world. The Museum, really a university, occupied a series of stately buildings surrounding a wide courtyard.

The library stood at the courtyard's head. Fifteen terraced stone steps, each the pale, dusty-rose color of the desert at sunset, led to the mighty columns which seemed to pierce the sky. The steps were worn smooth by the passing of thousands of sandals.

Library Director, Demetrius Phalereus (FAL-ler-e-us), a tall, thin man with the look of an accountant, waited amidst these columns for his assistant to return from the docks. A new shipment of papyrus scrolls had just arrived by ship today. Already the greatest collection of written wisdom, facts, history, information, theory, art, and drama in the world, Demetrius' library held almost 200,000 scrolls and would reach three times that number at its peak.

The assistant bounded up the steps, followed by a line of porters. "It's all here, Demetrius, scrolls, urns, even the paintings."

Demetrius smiled and nodded. This was a large shipment and had traveled far. He had feared damage or loss.

"But I have better news," continued his assistant. "Euclid (YEW-klid) has finished another book for us."

Euclid was a teacher and head of the museum's mathematics department.

Demetrius' eyes brightened. "Wonderful news! What's the topic of this book?"

"It is called *The Elements.*"

"The 'elements,' you say? *Which* elements? *What* elements?"

The staff assistant gazed toward a sapphire blue sky above trying to remember Euclid's words. One by one the porters filed past, lugging chests and crates. "As I recall, Euclid said that the elements are the most fundamental, basic theorems of mathematics, the ones required as the basis for the proof of other theorems. *The Elements* is in thirteen volumes and contains over 450 elements, or basic theorems."

"450 theorems," repeated Demetrius. "What exactly is a 'theorem' to be worth a whole book by our most famous mathematician?"

Again his assistant gazed skyward while he struggled to recall Euclid's words. "I think Euclid would say that a theorem is a basic relationship or truth which we can logically conclude about numbers, equations, or lines."

Demetrius slowly shook his head. "Theorems, equations . . . I can't understand this fascination with numbers. They're good for counting. But beyond that, I don't see the point."

"Have you attended any of his classes?" asked the assistant.

"I've never had the time."

"Euclid is the best teacher imaginable. I'm a poet, and he got *me* excited about geometry."

Demetrius shrugged. "I suppose that's why Ptolemy traveled to Athens to hire him. I, however, have better things to do than draw silly pictures of circles and triangles in the sand. *I* have a new shipment to examine."

Twenty-year-old Theoclese (THEE-oh-kleez) raced into his family's small house at the edge of their grain fields. This year's crops were planted. Green shoots sprouted everywhere repainting the dark brown dirt of their upper Nile Valley farm soft green. "Father! Father! I know what I must do."

"Do? You mean tomorrow morning when we start weeding?"

"No, father. I have been reading the most amazing book."

"Book?" Dentus exploded in anger. "You've been reading all day when you should have been in the fields?!" He slammed his fist on their rough wooden table. His voice thundered through the house. "I didn't teach you to read to dally away valuable work time!"

"But father, it's the most wonderful book imaginable." Theoclese had dropped to his knees, his hands resting on his father's thigh as he pleaded. "It's *The Elements*. Euclid explains everything about mathematics and geometry. I want to go to Alexandria . . . I *have* to go to Alexandria to study with Euclid."

Dentus tensed, his body rigid with shock, his voice now barely a whisper. "Alexandria is over thirty leagues away. You'd never be able to journey there, talk with this Euclid fellow, and be back to help run the farm."

Theoclese's voice now sounded stronger, more resolute. "No, father. I must leave the farm and become a full-time student at the Alexandria Museum. I must."

As if frozen in a stone etching the two remained motionless while this revelation slowly washed over and through the father. Finally Dentus' hand crept forward to rest on his son's shoulder. Dentus slowly shook his head, still bewildered by Theoclese's words. "My son, a mathematician. Who could have guessed?"

∾ ∾ ∾

White-bearded Euclid sat in his office in the museum, drumming his fingers on a wide, polished table that served as his desk. A scowl etched his usually kind face. "It's not right."

Two assistant professors sat with him, one, Leonara (Lee-oh-NAR-a), was the daughter of an Athens merchant, the other the nephew of an African prince.

Without looking up Euclid continued. "I've heard the rumors. I've seen the new students flocking in in droves. And it's not right!"

"What isn't right?" Leonara asked.

"They think *I* created the math concepts presented in *The Elements*. They give *me* the credit."

"It's an incredible work—logical, systematic, and comprehensive—and worthy of praise."

"But I didn't discover the theorems and axioms. I simply wrote a text-book. Certainly, I tried to write a complete and logical book, but . . ."

"Some of the *proofs* are yours," said the prince's nephew. "And the selection and organization of material is yours."

Euclid shook his head. "Yes, yes. But there are *giants* of mathematics who have come before—Hippocrates of Chios, Leon, Theudius of Magnesia, the Greeks Eudoxius, Aristeus, and Plato. *They* discovered the concepts. They deserve the praise of these students. I merely organized their work."

Leonara glanced out the window and down to the amphitheater Euclid used for his popular afternoon lectures. "Looks like over three hundred have already gathered for your afternoon class. Try convincing *them* you don't deserve the credit."

Euclid sighed, gathered his notes and rose. "I am just a teacher who wrote a textbook."

∽ ∽ ∽

The eager crowd rose and applauded when Euclid stepped into the amphitheater as if a famed dignitary had entered. Theoclese wedged himself into the front row and waved his copy of several volumes of *The Elements* as he cheered.

Euclid glared at the worshipping mob. "No! This is not right. I am a simple teacher. Applaud mathematics, not me."

But still they cheered and only quieted when Euclid began his lecture, so that they could soak in every word of this genius of mathematics who for many in the amphitheater had become the founder of logic and wisdom.

"There are five axioms, or basic assumptions which we must accept as true without proof. These are the foundation of the logic of mathematics. In previous lectures I have discussed three of these postulates: A straight line may be drawn connecting any two points; a straight line may be extended continuously in either direction; and, given two points, we can always draw a circle which will have one of the points as its center and will pass through the other."

The crowd sat in rapt attention, as if the very secrets of the universe were being whispered for their ears alone.

"From these axioms," continued Euclid, "all other theorems, and problem solutions are built. Today I will discuss the fourth of these basic postulates: All right angles are equal to one another."

Euclid paused and studied his students. They seemed more enchanted to be in his presence than to be unfolding the wonders of mathematics. Euclid shook his head and muttered, "Surely someone out there understands."

He raised his head and dutifully continued, "Right angles are a special and important angle, formed by the intersection of two perpendicular lines. Perpendicular lines may be defined as lines which cross each other in such a way that all four angles around their intersection are equal. Thus a right angle is exactly one-fourth part of a full circle."

The lecture continued. The crowd swelled to overflowing.

As Euclid concluded and started for the stage exit, many rushed to the stage begging just to touch the garment or sandal of the great mathematician. Still clutching his two volumes of *The Elements*, Theoclese was swept forward by the mob and smacked face to face into Euclid.

"Your book has changed my life," he stammered, gazing into Euclid's deep blue eyes.

"Let *mathematics* change your life. My book is just a guide to the mathematical genius discovered by others."

"No. It is you and your books that have inspired me," insisted Theoclese.

Euclid left still muttering, "I am only a teacher."

But Euclid was really much more than a simple teacher. His approach of logical, sequential, deductive reasoning, and the mathematical system he laid out in *The Elements* is still taught to every elementary and junior high school student today, 2300 years later. Euclid's five postulates, and especially his fifth postulate, form the basis of the geometry we all understand and use today, which we call "Euclidean Geometry."

With the exception of the Bible, no work has been more widely used, studied, and copied than Euclid's *The Elements*. More than a thousand editions of *The Elements* have been printed since its first printing in 1482. Countless more hand-printed copies were published before that date. For over two millennia this one set of books has defined our thinking and approach to the study of geometry. But our modern reliance on the work of this ancient Greek teacher is yet another story.

Follow-on Questions and Activities to Explore

1. Euclid was primarily concerned with geometry, with shapes, and with their relationships. His basic axioms all related to geometric construction. Are there similar basic postulates for arithmetic? What are they?

    Answer: There are two essential axioms for arithmetic. First is the identity of the set of whole numbers. Second is the relationship between adjacent numbers. (Each whole number is exactly one greater than the number before it and exactly one less than the number after it.)
    Basic algebra also requires that the number set be *ordered*. That is, if a>b, and b>c, then a>c; and if a = b, and b = c, then a = c.
    What do you think would happen to arithmetic and algebra if these basic axioms weren't necessarily true?

From *Marvels of Math*. © 1998 Kendall Haven. Teacher Ideas Press. (800) 237-6124.

"Flying" High

The Invention of Cartesian Coordinates
by René Descartes in the 1620s

At a Glance

René Descartes is best known as a seventeenth century philosopher. He is the one who first said, "I think, therefore I am." But Descartes also made important contributions to the fields of biology, physics, cosmology, and mathematics. Descartes' thinking, his approach to problem solving, came to dominate European thinking well into the eighteenth century.

Descartes is the one who gathered and promoted the use of the common arithmetic symbols we still use (=, +, -, ÷, etc.) But his most important mathematical contribution came in his successful effort to bridge the then very separate fields of geometry and algebra.

In the early seventeenth century, equations could not be graphed for study, and geometric curves and shapes, with the exception of a few, specific, well known shapes (circle, square, ellipse, etc.) couldn't be translated into algebraic form for detailed solution.

We call the merging of geometry and algebra "analytical geometry." It started with Descartes' idea to create a system of coordinates for graphs so that any point could be exactly described by its distance from the axes of the graph. Descartes got this brilliant idea from a fly.

Terms to Know

Understanding the following mathematical terms will help you understand and appreciate this story.

1. **Coordinates.** Coordinates tell us exactly where some point is relative to a set of base lines, or axes. Longitude and latitude form a coordinate system for the earth, telling us exactly where we are relative to the equator (north-south) and to 0 degrees longitude at Greenwich, England (east-west).

   For many geometry problems two axes are drawn at right angles to each other as the baselines for a graph. The position of any point on the graph can then be measured as so much distance from one axis, and so much distance from the other axis.

   No one had thought of how useful coordinates could be until the seventeenth century, when René Descartes invented them.

2. **Geometry.** Geometry is the study of points, lines, angles, surfaces, and solid shapes. During a geometry problem or study, we try to measure the properties, position, relative placement, and/or size of whatever is being studied.

   For several centuries there were only two fields of study under the general heading "mathematics." These were geometry and numerical studies which included arithmetic and algebra. Geometry and numerical studies were considered to be unrelated and totally separate until René Descartes created his Cartesian coordinate system.

3. **Algebra.** Algebra is the branch of mathematics which uses letters or symbols to represent unknown quantities and organizes problems into the form of equations. An equation is a statement of equality. One quantity or group of terms is stated to be equal to some other quantity or group of terms, and that equality is used to solve for the unknown value.

   Algebra uses the same four operations that are used in arithmetic plus squares, square roots (more generally, all exponential powers), and the six periodic functions to solve problems. Algebra allows us to solve much more complex problems than arithmetic.

   $x = 4 + 8$ is an example of a simple algebra problem.

"Flying" High

It was a time when wars raged across Europe. The Army of the Prince of Orange had just settled into winter camp for the rest of 1619. The dirt roads in the north of France were too muddy for an army to use. The rows of tents took on a permanent, built-in look around the houses and buildings the army had taken for its officers.

"Sergeant, see if Captain Descartes (Day-KART) is up."

"Doubt it sir. It's only 10 AM," answered the company duty sergeant snapping to attention, buttoning his heavy blue coat, and saluting all at the same time. But then, full colonels didn't drop into the company headquarters every day.

Irritated, the Colonel slapped his riding gloves against his starched white uniform pants. "The rest of the army rises at 6 . . ."

"Not Captain Descartes, sir. Never has. He was sickly as a child, sir. Sleeping in sort of became a habit."

The Colonel muttered, "If he weren't such a good soldier . . ." Again he slapped his thigh. "I must speak with him. Show me to his room."

Without knocking Colonel Gaspar shoved open the door and stepped into Descartes sparse room. Twenty-four-year-old René lay on his bed, one hand tucked behind his head.

Descartes neither moved nor stirred in surprise as his Colonel entered. He only smiled and said, "Welcome, Colonel. I have had the most amazing dream this morning."

Gaspar growled, "I need a meeting of all officers in the regiment at my headquarters at noon."

"*Today?*" asked Descartes, still lounging on his back. Though now stocky and muscular, René had been a frail youth. His nose formed a broad triangle above a wide, thin mouth. His eyebrows arched in the permanent look of a question. "At *noon?*"

"Yes, today!" snapped the Colonel as he turned to leave. "And you had better not be late."

From *Marvels of Math.* © 1998 Kendall Haven. Teacher Ideas Press. (800) 237-6124.

"But Colonel," called Descartes rising to sitting position, his curly hair tumbling across his shoulders. "I must tell you about my dream. It was . . . a message from heaven."

"From heaven, you say?" repeated Colonel Gaspar.

"I'm sure of it. It was far too vivid for an ordinary dream. Evil winds howled between church and school. A terrible storm battered the land. People shrieked and wailed for mercy. But I was not afraid. The storm could not hurt me. For in my hand, heaven had given me a key."

"A key," repeated the Colonel, growing increasingly fidgety as Descartes' story wore on. "What kind of key?"

"Sounds more like all the wine at the company party last night than a message from heaven to me," muttered the duty sergeant.

"It was the key to understanding all of nature," continued Descartes, gazing at his hand as if it still held that golden key.

"But what was it?" demanded Colonel Gaspar.

"The key was to use algebra and geometry together, to combine all of mathematics into a single system to understand the universe."

"Math, you say?" grunted the Colonel. "I say be at my headquarters at noon!" He spun on his well-polished boot heel and left.

"What do *you* think it means?" Descartes asked his staff sergeant.

"I'm just a simple soldier, sir. I wouldn't be knowin' about dreams."

"Use algebra and geometry together . . ." repeated Descartes. "What could it mean? There is no direct way to use one with the other. Everyone who has studied any mathematics knows that."

He flopped back onto his bunk and watched a fly lazily drone about the ceiling. "What could it mean? I *know* it's a message from God telling me what I must do with my life."

The fly buzzed in erratic patterns across the pealing plaster. "How can I combine geometry and algebra?" For just a moment it seemed to Descartes that the fly knew the answer as it buzzed, but wouldn't share.

From *Marvels of Math.* © 1998 Kendall Haven. Teacher Ideas Press. (800) 237-6124.

A year and a half later, René Descartes had shifted to the Bavarian army, which sat in winter camp less, and fought more. It was the bloody battle of Prague. It seemed that the army advanced into the city by inches, that each inch gained cost the lives of a hundred soldiers, and that each inch won was nothing but charred and crumpled ruin.

The Bavarian army had been stopped by a thick-walled section of the old-city fortifications. Cannons and muskets fired with deadly accuracy from behind the three-foot-thick walls of stone. Bavarian cannons tried to punch holes the soldiers could exploit. Nightly the defenders sneaked out to repair the damage. Periodically they would rush out during the day to push back the Bavarian cannons. The battle had raged before these walls for weeks.

It was an early afternoon in August of 1620. The Bavarian cannons were just roaring to life for the day. The troops waited, crouched behind bits of wall or old house, for either a chance to attack, or to repulse a counterattack.

Major Haflen commanded one section of the Bavarian artillery. "Cannons one through five," he screamed so as to be heard, "fire!"

The ground shook. Smoke and fire belched from five cannons simultaneously. The cannons bucked and rolled back. Five black cannon balls streaked through the afternoon sky and crashed into the fort. Rock and stone exploded away leaving a gap in the top of the wall.

The Bavarian troops cheered.

"Six through teeeenn. Load and prime! One through fiiiive, recover your piece."

"Major Haflen, a word please."

The major glanced over his shoulder. "Not now, Descartes. I'm rather busy."

Descartes' eager smile held the infectious enthusiasm of a child on Christmas morning. "I think you'll find this fascinating."

"Six through teeenn, fire!"

Thunder flashed out like a visible shock wave. Sulfur-rich smoke obscured the line of cannons. Returning cannon fire from the fort screeched toward Haflen's line and crashed into the soft ground sending out sprays of dirt and debris. Two cannoneers were hit by one shell and killed.

"Replacements forward for number threeee!"

"Major, the wheel on number four is loose again."

"Brace it and get that cannon back on line," barked Major Haflen. "One through fiiiive, load and prime!"

Descartes climbed the small knoll to stand next to the artillery major. Always fashionably dressed, René looked more prepared for tea than for battle. "I was lying on my cot this morning and realized that, and mind you, this is true for any regular three-dimensional solid . . ."

"One through fiiiive! fire!"

Outgoing shells belched fire, sulfur, blinding smoke, and a deafening roar. Incoming shells whined down with the squeal of death.

Descartes leaned closer so as to be heard over the din. "For all regular three-dimensional objects, it is true that the number of vertices, or corners, plus the number of faces, minus the number of edges, always equals two. Amazing! Always two—for *any* shape."

His face and uniform black with soot and grime, the major turned to stare at Descartes. "*That* is what you climbed up here in the middle of battle to tell me?"

"Don't you see? It's an algebraic expression that describes geometric shapes. It might be the beginning of my bridge between geometry and algebra."

Major Haflen shook his head and turned back to the line. "Six through teeenn! fire!"

Shouts and bugle calls erupted from the fort.

"They're attacking again!" cried a colonel, climbing the knoll beside Haflen and Descartes. He cupped his hands over his mouth and shouted back down to his officers, "Both regiments prepare to advance from the left! Fix bayonets!"

The Colonel grabbed Descartes arm. "And Captain, I hope your math studies won't be disrupted by a little fighting this afternoon."

"Not at all, sir," answered Descartes. "It's well past noon. My best thinking comes always in the morning as I lay in bed."

From *Marvels of Math.* © 1998 Kendall Haven. Teacher Ideas Press. (800) 237-6124.

On a sweltering, hazy morning six days later, René Descartes lounged on his bed. He watched a fly drift near the ceiling. It seemed as listless and lethargic in the muggy heat as Descartes felt.

Watching it, Descartes mused, "That fly is making sweeping arcs through the air, geometric shapes, and doesn't even know it."

Then with the first rumbling of a hint, Descartes thought, "If I could somehow measure, or describe, or identify, each point along that fly's path, I could write down an equation that would describe the arc."

Like the growing rumble of siege cannons, the idea seemed to vibrate through his being.

"If I could describe each point in *any* geometric shape, I could write an algebraic expression that would describe it."

The rumble rose to a thunderous roar inside his head.

"If I could do *that*, I would have found a way to use algebra to solve geometry, and a way to translate algebraic equations into geometry. That would be the key!"

Descartes bolted up in bed, intently watching the fly. How could he describe each point along the fly's wandering path? How could he do it in a way that would allow him to create an equation that would flow through those points?

The fly landed near an upper corner along the back wall, a few inches below the ceiling.

"Now it's easy to fix him," said Descartes. "He's three inches below the ceiling and about five inches from the side wall."

The fly buzzed off, bumping first into the ceiling, and then dipping toward the center of the room.

With a shock, Descartes realized he could describe any point the fly touched exactly as he had when it rested on the back wall. Any point in the room could be defined as so many inches from the ceiling, so many inches from the side wall, and so many inches from the back wall.

From *Marvels of Math.* © 1998 Kendall Haven. Teacher Ideas Press. (800) 237-6124.

Even better, he realized he didn't need to measure from whole surfaces, like walls. He could use lines as axes for a graph, like the three lines running out at right angles to each other from the upper corner of the room.

In a flash he saw all the space in the room marked off in a giant grid starting from those three lines, or axes. Every point in the room could be defined by its distance from those three axes.

Stealing a term from map makers, he called the distance of a point from each axis its "coordinates." The system he called "Cartesian coordinates." With these coordinates, any geometric shape or curve could be defined by a set of points, and could then be described as an algebraic equation. Any equation could be drawn as a geometric shape.

Geometry and algebra merged. The key to describing the universe had been found.

It was another twenty five years before René Descartes published his description of the natural world. His system of Cartesian coordinates to merge algebra and geometry was described in the third of three appendices of his philosophy book.

The branch of mathematics that uses the system René Descartes created we call "analytical geometry." For over three hundred years it has stood as one of the most powerful tools available to mathematicians to solve difficult problems. His system of coordinates is still one of the first elements of geometry any student learns.

And, it all came from watching a fly. Of course, whether the fly knew the secret all along is another story.

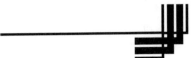

From *Marvels of Math.* © 1998 Kendall Haven. Teacher Ideas Press. (800) 237-6124.

Follow-on Questions and Activities to Explore

1. Coordinate systems are a means for determining position relative to fixed, known points or reference lines (axes). Try to design a new and unique coordinate system for your classroom. How many different ways can you and your classmates find?

   Answer: Here are four suggestions. See how many more you can create. 1) Like Descartes, you could define three walls as baselines and measure distance from those. 2) You could also use angles measured back to several fixed points to define position. (That is the system forest rangers use to locate forest fires.) 3) You could define position by saying which desks in the classroom you can touch from where you stand. 4) You could number all ceiling tiles and fix position by stating which tile you stood under.

2. For one week, keep a log of all the coordinate systems you see, use, or see others use. Write down what the system was used for and how it established coordinates to fix a location.

   Answer: Compare your answers to those of other students and discuss coordinate systems as a class. As hints, think of map grids, mileage tables, longitude and latitude, chess boards, and math class problems. Use your school and public library and the Internet to search for more coordinate systems.

Shadow Boxing

The Invention of Perspective Geometry
by Girard Desargues in 1635

At a Glance

Humans have always drawn images, likenesses, of things around them. Many of these early drawings of buildings and landscapes seem crude to us because they aren't drawn in perspective. That is, they aren't drawn to look on paper the way the actual scene looks to our eye.

It is not that early humans couldn't draw. It is that they hadn't learned about perspective drawing.

What is perspective drawing? Imagine that you were going to draw a picture of two men, both exactly six feet tall. If one man were a few feet from you and the other a hundred feet away, you would draw the near man taller in your picture, even though they are both the same height. That's how they appear to your eye. And that is perspective drawing.

Stand on a bridge overlooking a long, straight road. The road seems to grow narrower in the distance until the two sides, which you know are really parallel, seem to touch, closing off the road.

This is also perspective, the way your eye sees the world.

But for a very long time no one knew how to translate three-dimensional objects into two-dimensional drawings so that they would look "right" to the viewer. That is, no one knew how to draw in perspective and still be exactly true to the detailed measurements of the object being drawn.

Then Girard Desargues recognized the obvious, and our ability to use perspective geometry and mechanical drawing began.

Terms to Know

Understanding the following mathematical terms will help you understand and appreciate this story.

1. **Perspective.** Perspective is the art and science of representing three-dimensional, solid objects on a flat drawing so that they seem to be in correct relation to one another just as the human eye sees them.

Perspective means that something very close will be drawn as bigger than something of the same size that is farther away. This is not done because things actually get smaller as they move away, but because they *appear* to grow smaller. It is the perspective the human eye sees.

The parallel sides of a road appear to edge closer and closer together in the distance until they seem to meet. We know they really don't. But that's the way it looks to a human eye. So that's the way we draw them when making a perspective drawing.

2. **Three-Dimensional.** We are each three-dimensional objects. So is everyone and everything in our world. We have named those three dimensions length, depth, and height. Everything you touch, feel, use, or own will have all three of these dimensions.

3. **Two-Dimensional.** Drawings and paintings are two-dimensional. They have length and height, but no depth. They are on the flat surface of a piece of paper. The paper, itself, of course, *does* have depth. It is a three-dimensional object. But the drawing made on its surface has only two dimensions.

Almost every drawing and painting you will ever make is an attempt to make a two-dimensional drawing appear like some three-dimensional object or scene. We learn perspective and other graphic tricks to place and draw objects on our two-dimensional figures so that they will look to the human eye the same as they would if those same eyes directly viewed the three-dimensional object.

Shadow Boxing

The afternoon rain had ended. As the sun set on March 21, 1628, Lieutenant Girard Desargues (Day-ZARG) could find no dry place to sit. A deep chill settled over the French army encampment as the last rays of sunset sparkled with a golden glow. Far too thin and delicate to match the image of a rugged army officer, Desargues was an architect and engineer. His passion and hobby was mathematics.

Beside him sat Major René Descartes, already famed as one of the great mathematicians of the century. Before them stood the towering walls of La Rochelle, France.

It seemed somehow comical to Desargues that two armies could sit several hundred yards apart for almost a year and never meet, allowing a single, twenty-foot high wall to keep them apart. For almost a year the two great armies had concentrated on either tearing down, or on building up that wall (depending on whether you sat on the inside or outside), instead of on fighting over open fields as armies were supposed to do. But each night the cold and mud sank into Desargues' bones and the deafening roar of siege cannons hammered his ears and he lost sight of anything comical.

As the sun set and evening torches were lit in the army camp, Desargues and Descartes were discussing, almost arguing, over a crude drawing on Desargues, lap.

"Look again, René," said Desargues. "If I draw a picture of a man six feet tall standing in front of a wall that is twenty feet tall, and the man stands eight feet from me (as that guard now stands), and the wall is—what would you say?—one hundred and twenty feet from me (as the La Rochelle wall is now), then in my drawing how tall should I draw the wall, and how tall should I make the man?"

Without waiting for an answer, Desargues sketched the man with feet near the bottom of his piece of paper and head near the top. Far behind this figure, Desargues drew the wall with both top and bottom near the middle of the page. "In my drawing, the man has to be taller. Does that not look correct? Is that not what your eye sees?"

From *Marvels of Math.* © 1998 Kendall Haven. Teacher Ideas Press. (800) 237-6124.

"As a mere picture, it may *look* correct," answered Descartes. "But mathematically it is very incorrect. The wall must be over three times as tall as the man."

"Why?" demanded Desargues. "The wall must look smaller because it is farther away."

"It must be taller because that is the correct height for the wall."

"But is that what your eye sees?"

"It is what is mathematically correct."

Desargues shook his head. "Why must mathematics look so wrong?"

"Mathematics must be precise," answered the major. "If the man is six feet tall, then his height in the picture must be that height that represents six feet. The wall must be the height that represents twenty feet. Otherwise the drawing contains no reliable, useful information."

"But it would *look* wrong."

"But it would *be* precise and correct."

The great siege guns erupted with the first volley of the night's bombardment. Fire belched into the night as if from an exploding volcano or seething blast furnace. The ground shook. The shock waves and thunderous roar knocked the breath out of anyone within one hundred feet. The air filled with sulfurous smoke that stung the eyes and nose. Rock and mortar were ripped from La Rochelle's walls and sprayed across the fields, the same rock which defenders had spent all day rebuilding.

Further conversation was impossible. Desargues and Descartes drifted apart, the unsettled question still lingering in the air between them.

Seven years later, in 1635 and out of the army, Girard Desargues had returned to his native Lyons in southern France as a successful architect. But the problem he had presented to Descartes still tormented him.

In late October Desargues sat with a merchant friend, Ives Tillest, in one of the new tea houses in Lyons. Tea had been introduced into Paris for the first time earlier that year and had quickly spread to other French cities. The first chill of winter hung like a bitter warning in the air. The glory of fall lay behind them like a fading dream.

Ives Tillest wrinkled up his face at his first sip of tea. "It's too bitter!"

Desargues laughed. "You have to get use to it, Ives. Add cream and sugar." But even as he spoke Desargues did not look at his friend. Rather he stared at a small box on the table between them. "Look at the shadow of this cube, Ives."

"This *what?*" interrupted Tillest.

"This box. See how much bigger the shadow is than the actual side of the box?"

"The sun is low in the sky," answered Ives.

Desargues pointed at the shadow. "In mathematical terms, is not that shadow really a two-dimensional representation, a two-dimensional *transformation*, of the three-dimensional cube?"

Tillest shrugged. "It's just a shadow."

Desargues shook his head. "Do you not agree that the shadow's exact shape is determined by the box?"

"Yes, of course. It's the box's shadow."

"That shadow is now long and faces east. But if we had been here at noon, when the same shadow would have been very small and faced north, wouldn't you have also recognized it as the shadow of this same box?"

Again Tillest grimaced as he forced down another sip of tea. "Ghastly stuff. It will never catch on. And, yes, of course I would recognize a box's shadow at any time of day."

"My point exactly," smiled Desargues, slamming his hands onto the table for emphasis so that the box and both tea cups jumped. Tillest's cup tipped over as it crashed back onto its saucer.

Desargues leaned forward with his napkin. "I'm so sorry. I'll get you another cup."

"No, don't bother. I think I'll have something else."

Desargues' thoughts returned to the box. "No matter what direction or size the shadow is, we would still know it came from the same box. If the shadow grew bigger, we would not think the box grew bigger. Rather we would know that the source of the light rays creating the shadow had been lowered."

Tillest dabbed at the spilled tea with his napkin as he shook his head at his friend. "And what, pray tell, is your point in all that?"

Desargues laughed. "A thousand pardons, Ives. But you are not a mathematician, and have not been told the opposite by countless other mathematicians for all your life."

"Mathematicians claim they can't recognize a box's shadow?" interrupted Tillest. "They're worse off than I thought."

But Desargues had turned serious, leaning forward, gesturing forcefully. "They claim that if I do not draw each object in exact proportion to its size regardless of its position in the picture, we can know *nothing* about the object being drawn, whether it looks right or not."

"You'd know what it *looks* like," offered Tillest.

Desargues continued, "In my heart I know they are wrong. I know there must be a way to make drawings of three-dimensional objects look correct and still be mathematically precise." Then he sighed. "It's as if the answer is hiding there in that shadow before me. I know it's there, but I just can't see it."

∾ ∾ ∾

A week later at home during a rain storm, Desargues brooded in his study. Gusts of strong wind whistled around the window panes and sent the candle flames wavering, causing shadows to race across the wall.

The answer is there in the shadows. "But where?" he cried, pounding his fist.

Without even being quite sure what he planned to do, Desargues rummaged through a closet until he found a small, cubical box. He placed it on a table directly in front of a candle. A heavy shadow spread out from the box toward the far wall.

Suddenly Desargues saw what had been right under his nose all along. Even though the sides of his box were straight and parallel, the sides of its shadow spread out at an angle as the shadow stretched toward the wall. A six-inch-wide box cast a three-foot-wide shadow on the wall.

Desargues slid the box toward the candle. The angle of the shadow's sides increased. The shadow on the wall grew wider. He slid the box away from the candle. The angle of the shadow's sides decreased. The shadow shrank.

The idea burst into his head. *Of course* mathematically correct didn't look right. Mathematics and the real world worked on two different assumptions. Geometry, as defined by Euclid, assumed that parallel lines never meet. They stay exactly parallel forever. That was the definition of parallel.

But in the real world light didn't follow that rule. All light spread out from single points—a candle or the sun. Light expanded in straight lines, but they weren't parallel lines. Similarly, in order for the human eye to see, light beams had to converge on it from every object in the eye's field of vision.

The lines that the eye saw were not Euclid's parallel lines. The eye saw along lines that converged at a point, the eye, and spread out from there.

The idea was so simple, so obvious, Desargues almost couldn't believe it. In order to make his drawings *look* right, he had only to change the basic assumption he used. Instead of Euclid's assumption, Desargues would use a new assumption for his drawings, one that matched what the eye actually saw.

Desargues would now assume that parallel lines *do* meet—at a point on the distant horizon.

Desargues felt giddy with light-headed elation. At last, an answer! He began to dance around the room throwing his own wild shadow dancing across the walls.

Then the questions and doubts flooded in. Would this idea work? Would it allow for precise measurement on the drawing? How would he use this new assumption, this new concept?

From *Marvels of Math.* © 1998 Kendall Haven. Teacher Ideas Press. (800) 237-6124.

43-3856 Orig

Travis, David. **Paris: photographs from a time that was.** Art Institute of Chicago/Yale, 2005. 100p ISBN 0300113935, $24.95

This book was released in conjunction with an exhibition organized at and by the Art Institute of Chicago in fall 2005. Travis, the exhibition curator and the institute's photography curator, selected the works from the Art Institute's collection. He also wrote an 18-page in-depth essay, "Paris: Photographs from a Time That Was," as an introduction to the book and its 72 reproductions of black-and-white photographs. The organizing element of the exhibition and the book is obviously Paris and the many photographers who used "the city as subject matter and backdrop" to establish their style and sometimes their best works. Although the author mentions a "new generation's acceptance and celebration of the fluidity of the city's street life focused on time as a new element in making photographs," the considered period spans more than a century, beginning with a photograph by Mestral (1851) and ending with one signed by Cartier-Bresson in 1957. Baudelaire and his celebrated *flâneur* had lived through rough times by then, and Walter Benjamin had committed suicide in Portbou in order to escape French/German deportation. **Summing Up:** Highly recommended. All levels.—*B. P. Chalifour, SUNY College at Brockport*

QA21. H32. 1998

(Marvels of Math

Desargues sank back into his desk chair and pulled out a piece of drawing paper. *Parallel lines meet at a point on the distant horizon.* Desargues drew a horizon line and placed a dot on it—the point where parallel lines meet. He called this point a *vanishing* point because spaces (like ribbons of road) seemed to vanish when they reached that spot.

Desargues decided to test his new system by drawing three boxes, one in front and two farther back. He drew the front face of the front box and drew lines from each corner back to the vanishing point. In three minutes he had drawn all three boxes.

It was simple. It was precise. And it looked right! It looked exactly like what the human eye saw and still allowed for precise mathematical measurement.

Girard Desargues was overjoyed. He bubbled over with excitement for months and could talk of little else than what he called his new projective geometry.

He quickly wrote a small book, *Brouillon Project*, and published it, expecting rave reviews, universal acclaim, and fame.

His book was ignored. No one read it. No one commented. No one cared.

The book, and Desargues' projective geometry were forgotten for almost two hundred years before Michael Charles found a hand-written copy in a back storage room of a Paris library. By the mid-nineteenth century people were ready to recognize the value and brilliance of Desargues' work. It was an "instant" rave success. In the twentieth century, Desargues' projective geometry has expanded into a whole new field of quantitative geometric study. But how that field of study has touched our modern lives is another story.

From *Marvels of Math.* © 1998 Kendall Haven. Teacher Ideas Press. (800) 237-6124.

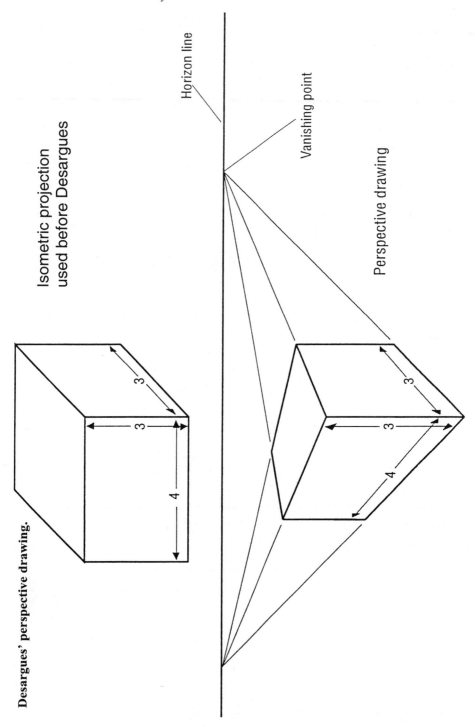

Isometric projection
used before Desargues

Horizon line

Vanishing point

Perspective drawing

Desargues' perspective drawing.

Follow-on Questions and Activities to Explore

1. Darken the room except for one light source—a flashlight, candle, or ordinary light bulb. Move some object (about five or six inches in size) forward and back, and side to side in front of the light source. How does the object's shadow change? Study the shadow closely. Does its shape change as well as its size? Do the angles between sides and top appear to change? Do the relative proportions of its various parts change?

   Now move the same object relative to your eye. Come in close, move it farther away. View it from on top and underneath. How did the look, the appearance, of your object change? Do parallel lines always look parallel? Do they sometimes appear to angle away from each other?

   If you were to draw a picture of this object, what perspective would you use? What would make it look most correct?

   Answer: Compare your answer with those of other students and discuss it as a class.

2. On a piece of paper draw two simple boxes, one with and one without the aid of a vanishing point as created by Girard Desargues. Use a ruler and straight edge to make your boxes as exact as possible. Which box looks more correct to your eye? Why?

   Answer: Compare your answer with those of other students and discuss it as a class.

Stories
About
Mathematical
Concepts

The Weighing Game

The Invention of
Specific Gravity and Buoyancy
by Archimedes in 232 BC

At a Glance

Archimedes, a mathematician, scientist, and inventor lived on the island of Sicily in the Mediterranean Sea. He is considered by most scholars to be one of the five greatest mathematicians of all time along with Newton, Einstein, Galileo, and Gauss. Archimedes' inventions and discoveries touch each of our lives, over two thousand years after his death. They include the lever, corkscrew water pump, catapult, and buoyancy among a long list.

There are many great stories about Archimedes, probably more than about any other mathematician in history—his counting the grains of sand on the beach, the discovery of the lever, how he defended the city of Syracuse from the Roman army, etc. Here is one story about this great person.

Terms to Know

Understanding the following mathematical terms will help you understand and appreciate this story.

1. **Inscribe.** Literally, the word inscribe means to draw one geometric shape inside another so that they touch at certain points along their boundary. What that practically means is that the shape being inscribed inside another must be *as big as possible* without spilling over the edge of the larger shape.

    If a circle is inscribed inside a square, the circle will touch the square at the center of each side of the square. If it were any bigger, it would stretch outside the square. If it were any smaller, it wouldn't touch on all four sides, and could be bigger.

    If a square is inscribed inside a circle, each of the square's four corners will touch the circle.

2. **Circumscribe.** Circumscribe is the opposite of inscribe. A circumscribed shape will surround all sides of some other shape, but must be as small as possible without shrinking inside the other shape. Circumscribing a square around a circle is the same as inscribing the circle within that square.

   The key to both inscribing and circumscribing is that the shapes must be as close to the same size as possible. It is very much like trying to fit a hand inside a glove. Inscribing refers to fitting the biggest possible hand inside a given glove. Circumscribing refers to fitting the smallest possible glove over a given hand.

3. **Right Triangle.** A triangle is a shape made of three straight sides. The two lines meeting at each corner of a triangle form an angle between 0 degrees and 180 degrees. If one of those angles is exactly 90 degrees, the triangle is called a "right triangle" since 90 degrees is called a "right angle."

   Many special and interesting relationships exist for the sides and angles of a right triangle which have made them a focal point of geometric study since the time of the earliest Greek mathematicians.

4. **Cylinder.** A cylinder is a three-dimensional object that is round (circular) on both ends and has straight sides. A tube is a cylinder. A section of pipe is a cylinder. From the end a cylinder looks like a circle. From the side it looks like a rectangle.

5. **Sphere.** A sphere is a three-dimensional circle. Any round ball is a sphere. The earth is a very slightly lopsided sphere.

6. **Cone.** A cone is circular at one end, and tapers down to a point at the other end. An ice-cream cone is shaped like a cone. If a pyramid were made round instead of rectangular at its base, it would be a cone.

The Weighing Game

On the smooth dirt floor of his modest house along a road climbing one of the steep hills leading away from Syracuse harbor on the island of Sicily, 54-year-old Archimedes (Ar-ki-MEE-deez), began to draw with a small stick. The house was not as near the sparkling beach or bustling port of the walled city of Syracuse as Archimedes would have liked. But the famous, gray haired "miracle" mathematician had little time to waste thinking on such matters.

"If I draw a square, and inscribe a circle just inside that square, they will have the same center point. Also the circle will touch the square at the midpoint of each of its sides. . . . What next?"

His stick paused as his mind raced. He concentrated so hard, he couldn't tell if seconds or hours passed before a notion of how to proceed crept into his mind.

"What if I add a right triangle with the point of the right angle just touching the center of the top of the square and a height equal to the height of the square?"

His stick carefully traced new lines in the smoothly raked and swept dirt. He leaned back in his low chair to study the drawing.

"These are all flat, two-dimensional shapes. But what if, in my mind, I spin them around on their common vertical axis to form a cone, a cylinder, and a sphere, or ball?"

"Archimedes! Archimedes!"

Archimedes eyes closed as he pictured the three-dimensional shapes floating in his mind. "Then the sphere would be entirely inside the cylinder, and the cone would be. . ."

"Archimedes!" This time the voice shouted right in his ear. A messenger in sparkling white silk and gold trim leaned over, gently shaking his shoulder. "Archimedes! I have been knocking and calling from your door for ten minutes."

Archimedes frowned, trying not to let this intrusion force the shapes from his mind. "Don't stand on my drawings. Go away!"

From *Marvels of Math.* © 1998 Kendall Haven. Teacher Ideas Press. (800) 237-6124.

"But Archimedes. King Hieron has sent for you."

With a deep sigh, Archimedes let the floating shapes fade from his mind's eye. He turned to glare at the messenger. "You are interrupting important work!"

Archimedes stood thin and tall, with a full head of wild, gray hair, a thick, curly beard, and a habit of glaring at people when he spoke, as if seething with anger. All in all, he was an imposing figure. His fame as the greatest mathematician of all time added an aura of mystical wonder to his wild appearance.

Embarrassed by Archimedes' gruff reply, the messenger repeated, "King Hieron has sent for you."

"What does he want?" snapped Archimedes. "My work here is very important."

Not knowing what else to say, the messenger repeated, "King Hieron wants—you." Then he added, gazing at the geometric floor drawings, "What are you working on?"

"I am attempting to calculate the volume of a sphere."

The messenger thought for a moment and then suggested, "Why not fill the sphere with water, and then pour the water into a square tub, so you can measure how much water the sphere held? That will tell you its volume."

The messenger smugly smiled at having been able to offer such a brilliant plan to the great Archimedes.

Archimedes glared out of the corner of one eye as he wearily rose. "That would tell me the volume of only *one* sphere. I must discover a way to calculate the volume of *every* sphere."

"Why?"

Archimedes waved a hand in disgust. "Go away and leave me alone!"

"But—but King Hieron has summoned you."

Archimedes was well known as a loner, a thinker, almost a hermit. He was also known to be the most brilliant and clever mathematician anyone in Syracuse, Rome, Alexandria, Greece, or Carthage had ever heard of. Born the son of a famed astronomer, Archimedes studied in the great schools of Alexandria before returning to his native Syracuse.

Archimedes and the messenger stepped into a beautiful spring afternoon in the year 232 BC. Archimedes seemed surprised. "It's late afternoon already! I would have guessed mid-morning."

Birds chirped and swooped over gracious public buildings of marble and granite. Fountains bubbled into long, quiet reflecting pools. Trees were draped in pink and white blankets of blossoms. The sweet air smelled of the sea, of honeysuckle, and of the grand open-air market.

King Hieron dismissed even his closest advisors when Archimedes was announced. Though many in the court protested loudly, guards soon cleared the grand room and closed the double doors behind them with a resounding "thud!" that echoed across the long, empty space.

Alone in the vast room, King Hieron led Archimedes to a small table beside his throne. Unfolding a rich, velvet cloth he exposed a shining crown, a head-wreath, made of purest gold. Its dazzling reflection in the afternoon rays made Archimedes squint.

"It is magnificent, my king."

King Hieron nodded sourly. "Perhaps . . ." He picked up the wreath, seemingly examining its every detail. "But is it what I ordered?"

The king paused with arched eyebrows, as if hoping Archimedes could anticipate his question and answer it already. "You see, I gave a local goldsmith an amount of gold and asked him to fashion it into a crown of this design. But now I fear he has cheated me and wrapped a thin layer of gold around some other, cheaper metal inside."

King Hieron turned back to Archimedes, holding out the shining crown. "How can I be sure the crown is really pure gold?"

"I presume you aren't willing to make a tiny cut through one or two of the leaves to see . . ."

"Never!" bellowed the king. "If it *is* pure gold, the cuts would ruin its perfection and show that I do not trust the craftsmen of this city."

Archimedes paused in thought, his eyes gazing off toward the distant horizon, his face wrinkled in concentration. "I also presume you have weighed the crown, and that its weight matches the weight of gold you gave to the goldsmith?"

The king nodded. "It matches exactly."

"Interesting . . ." murmured Archimedes, stroking his beard. "How can I tell what is inside without looking inside?"

"Well?" insisted the king. "How can I?"

"I will have to give the matter some thought."

The king looked forlorn as Archimedes left without offering an answer.

The next morning a uniformed Captain of the Guard and a line of five armed soldiers marched into Archimedes' house and found him sitting on the dirt floor studying his drawings.

"What if I cut a very thin slice through all three shapes, the cylinder, the sphere, and the cone somewhere below the mid-point of the cylinder's side? As I cut slices closer and closer to the bottom, the cone's area grows bigger as the sphere's grows smaller. . . . But what is the relationship?"

"Archimedes! I have come for your answer to the king's question."

Archimedes struggled to hold the shapes and slices in his mind. "Get out of my light and leave me alone!"

The Captain said, "You are supposed to be solving the *King's* problem."

"But can't you see how much more important it is for me to spend my time and energy on pure mathematics?"

"What is important is to do what your king bids you to do."

"Very well," sighed Archimedes, again allowing the images in his mind to slowly fade away. "Tell King Hieron I will find his answer. Now leave me alone!"

At the door the Captain paused. "The king wants his answer *today*!"

Unable to muster any enthusiasm for a frivolous material problem (like whether a crown was made of pure gold or not) when there were so many mighty problems of mathematics and geometry that needed solving, Archimedes wandered to one of the public bath houses. He climbed into one of the

---

heated tubs and lounged back, closing his eyes, picturing spheres, cylinders—and leafy gold crowns.

He lazily opened one eye and noticed his hand and arm floating on the water's surface. A vague, still unformed thought began to emerge in the back of his mind. He pulled his arm completely under the surface. Then he relaxed and it floated back up. He pulled the arm down. It floated back up.

A powerful thought, an idea, clattered around his mind like a runaway horse. But it remained vague, unshaped, undefined. Something important was happening before his eyes. But what?

He stood up in the tub. The water level dropped around the tub's sides. He sat back down. The water level rose. He stood. It fell. He sat. It rose.

He lay all the way down so that just his nose and eyes were above water. The water rose higher, and he felt lighter! The key elements of the idea began to form.

He stood up. The water level fell and he felt heavier. He lay down. The water rose and he felt lighter.

The idea snapped into focus as a wondrous relationship between the weight and volume of water, and the weight and volume of an object placed in water.

Dripping water across the tile floor, Archimedes ran to the bath house garden and retrieved several large rocks.

Back in the tub, he held one of the rocks in his hand to get a feel for its weight. Then he lowered it under the water. The water level inched up the tub's sides. The rock felt lighter.

"I have found it!" he cried. "I have found it!" (Of course, in his language, the word for "I have found it," was "Eureka!," Archimedes' famous cry.)

Forgetting all else, Archimedes dashed toward the king's palace. "Eureka!"

"Archimedes!" called the bath house attendant. "You forgot your clothes!"

"The answer is simple," Archimedes announced to King Hieron. "The key is the *density* of matter."

The king could sense Archimedes excitement and didn't mind that he forgot to add a "your majesty."

"What is this density?" asked the king.

"Density is a measure of how much weight of material is packed into each small volume of a substance. Gold is very dense. It has a great weight, or mass, per cubic inch. Feathers have a low density. There is little weight in a cubic inch of feathers."

"I understand," interrupted the king. "But how does that solve my problem?"

"Gold is heavier, more dense, than other metals, my king. So that it will take a greater volume of other metals to make the same weight. If the crown is not pure gold, its total volume will be greater than that for an equal weight of gold."

The king demanded, "But how can I measure the volume of this crown without melting it down into a solid cube?"

Archimedes smiled. "Water, my king. Place the crown in water and we will compare the amount of water it displaces to the amount of water an equal weight of gold will displace. If the crown displaces more water, its volume must be bigger, which means it cannot be pure gold."

With a simple bowl of water the cheating goldsmith was caught and Archimedes' position as royal hero was again confirmed.

"Maybe now everyone will leave me alone so I can solve some real problems!"

When Archimedes finally reasoned out a formula for the volume of a sphere, he called it his greatest accomplishment. In fact, when he died, he had the image of a sphere inscribed inside a cylinder carved onto his tombstone. His efforts to define the volumes of various geometric shapes, and his efforts to calculate a more exact value for π were not measurably improved upon for two thousand years. But making those improvements is another story.

Follow-on Questions and Activities to Explore

1. Why do you feel lighter in water? Why can you float on water and not on air?

   Answer: The answer lies in the density of things. Density is a measure of how much mass is packed into every unit volume of a substance, or how heavy every cubic inch of the stuff is. Really it is a measure of how hard the earth is pulling on each tiny bit of an object, trying to pull it toward the center of the earth.

   Actually all gasses and liquids push *up* on you when you are in them. Air does. So does water. They are trying to push you out of the way and follow the pull of gravity closer to the center of the earth. The denser the gas or liquid, the more it is able to push up on you, so the lighter you feel.

   Your body has almost the same density as water. It pushes up on you almost as hard as gravity pulls you down. Very salty water (Great Salt Lake in Utah, for example) is more dense than either fresh or ocean water, and is more dense than the average human body. Most people find it hard to sink under the surface of Great Salt Lake even when they try.

2. Let's test Archimedes buoyancy and density principle. Find a rock (or rocks) that weigh the same as a handy piece of wood. Which looks bigger to you? Which do you think is more dense? Why?

   Fill a bowl 2/3 full with water. Be sure the bowl is big enough, and that the water is deep enough to submerge first the rock(s) and then the piece of wood without overflowing.

   Wait for all ripples and waves to die out in the water and mark the water level in the bowl with a grease pencil or waterproof marker. Submerge the rock(s) and mark how high the water rises—how much water the rock(s) displace(s).

   Remove the rock(s) and submerge the piece of wood. The wood will float so you will have to hold it down with a pencil or nail. Mark how high the water rose this time (how much water the wood displaced).

   Which displaced more water? Which was more dense? What's the hardest part of doing this type of experiment accurately?

   Answer: Compare your answer with other students and discuss the experiment as a class.

3. Archimedes was trying to determine the volume of a sphere by inscribing it inside other geometric shapes and by circumscribing it around others. Let's see if that technique works.

   Pretend that you don't know how to find the area of a circle. How could you make a good guess at that area? Try inscribing one square inside the circle, and circumscribing a second square around the circle. The area of the circle will have to be between these two areas. (Halfway between will be a good guess.)

   Call the radius of the circle "1 unit." The figure on page 82 shows the circle and the inscribed and circumscribed squares. It also includes samples of the calculations you will have to make.

   Answer: Compare your answer and drawings with those of other students and discuss the process as a class.

Estimating area with inscribed and circumscribed shapes.

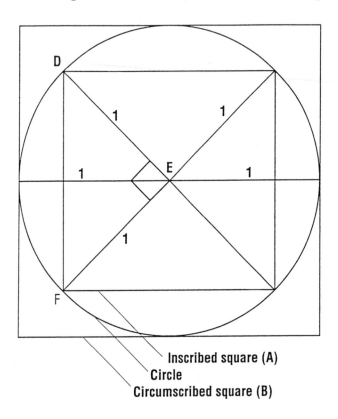

Inscribed square (A)
Circle
Circumscribed square (B)

- Let circle radius = 1
- Then each side of square (B) = 2
- Each side of square (A) must be calculated
  In triangle DEF, sides DE & EF = 1
  From the Pythagorean Theorem, side $DF^2 = 1^2 + 1^2 = 1 + 1 = 2$, so DF $= \sqrt{2}$
- Area of square (B) = $2^2 = 4$
- Area of square (A) $= \sqrt{2}^2 = 2$

The area of the circle must lie between the area of these two squares.
A good guess would be halfway between, or 3.

Actual area of circle $= \pi r^2 = (3.14)(1^2) = 3.14...$so 3 was a good guess!

The Odds Are . . .

*The Invention of Probability Theory
by Pierre de Fermat in 1654*

At a Glance

Humans have always played games, including betting or gambling games. Early written and pictograph records from Babylonian, Greek, Roman, and Egyptian societies all show the existence of dice-like betting games. Instead of our modern plastic dice, they used a small, generally cubic ankle bone, the astragalus bone, of large game animals.

Even though all these early cultures gambled at dice games, none of their respective mathematicians ever thought about, or tried to predict, the odds (or probability) of winning such a game until well into the seventeenth century. The first to seriously attack the problem were two French mathematicians in the mid-1600s—Blaise Pascal, a full-time professional mathematician, and Pierre de Fermat, a lawyer and enthusiastic amateur mathematician. A friendly contest blossomed between the two to see who would first develop a working theory on the probability of winning a betting game.

Pierre de Fermat, the amateur, won and was the first to develop a theory of probability. But it is not that important theory, but a tormenting and tantalizing mathematical puzzle Fermat left behind for which he is best known.

Terms to Know

Understanding the following mathematical terms will help you understand and appreciate this story.

1. **Theorem.** A theorem is the statement of a rule or relationship expressed in terms of mathematical symbols and equations. Pythagoras' famous theorem tells us about the relationship of the length of the sides of a certain kind of triangle and is written $a^2 + b^2 = c^2$.

    Theorems can be proposed at any time, but must be proved in order to be of general use. It is often much easier to see that a relationship *seems* to always be true and express it as a theorem, than it is to *prove* that it must *always* be true.

2. **Prime Number.** A prime number is a whole number that cannot be evenly divided by any whole number other than by itself and by one. 1, 3, 5, 7, 11, 13, 17, 19, and 23 are all prime numbers. Prime numbers have always fascinated mathematicians. The early Greeks gave great significance to prime numbers and studied them exhaustively. Pierre de Fermat was also fascinated by prime numbers, and especially by their relationships with other numbers. Many of his theorems describe the relationship between prime numbers, and between prime and non-prime numbers.

3. **Proof.** To prove something is to demonstrate that it *must* be true. Proofs are used in all fields of math. Beginning with known truths and factual relationships, a proof tries to logically show that some new concept or theorem must also always be true.

4. **Probability.** Probability is a measure of how likely an occurrence is to happen. It is very likely that you will live long enough to take another breath. The probability of this occurring is almost 100 percent. It is very unlikely that you will live to be 150 years old. The probability of that occurring is almost 0 percent.

   Probability is usually expressed as either a percentage chance of occurring (John has a 40 percent probability of getting a hit next time he is at bat) or as a ratio (The odds are 2 to 5 that John gets a hit next time he's at bat).

   Probability is an important concept for gambling. Every gambler wants to know the odds (or probability) of winning before they bet. Pierre de Fermat opened the door to calculating that probability.

The Odds Are . . .

September 24, 1654

Dear Pierre,

You are most cruel, you rascal. This last problem you challenged me to solve is exceedingly cunning. Do you stay up late at night to invent such torments for your friends?

I know, Pierre, you are fascinated by prime numbers and their unique properties. But this time you have outdone yourself! You asked me to prove that if p is a prime number, and if some other number, r, cannot be evenly divided into p, then r raised to the p-1 power, all minus 1 ($r^{p-1}-1$) will always be divisible by p.

I have tried 100 examples and can see that it works. But to prove it. . . . How about one clue, or hint to ease the turmoil of my mind?

Fondly,

Frenicle de Bessy

~ ~ ~

Pierre de Fermat (pee-AIR day fer-MAH) chuckled and adjusted the lantern he used for a reading light as he reread the letter. "Never will I give you a hint, you old dog. Squirm on the end of my mathematical skewer until you figure it out for yourself as I have!"

Again he chuckled, harder this time, at the pure joy of the endless world of mathematical puzzles. Then his long face clouded as he glanced at a second letter that lay on his desk delivered earlier this day in the fall of 1654. His large, dark eyes tightened. His hand squeezed into a fist and pounded his desk.

This second letter was from Blaise Pascal. Pascal was getting close. Fermat and Pascal had been corresponding for over six months as they each tried to solve the mystery of discovering a way to correctly predicting the probability of winning a game of chance, like dice. That is, a method that would match actual observation.

"Are you ever coming to bed?" Fermat's wife called from the top of the stairs.

From *Marvels of Math.* © 1998 Kendall Haven. Teacher Ideas Press. (800) 237-6124.

"In a bit, Louise."

Fermat could hear her footsteps start down the stairs. "Are you preparing your case for tomorrow?"

"I'll be up in a bit. You go on to bed."

Carrying a candle whose light spilled out before her, Louise, Fermat's wife of twenty years, stepped into his study. "I know it's an important case you argue tomorrow. But you need your . . ." She stopped mid-sentence as she came close enough to see the papers scattered across her husband's desk. Her voice slid toward irritation. "You're playing with math, aren't you?"

Defensively Fermat slid his math papers under a law book. "Why do you say that?"

Louise accusingly shook a finger at him. "A man's life hangs in the balance on how well you argue your case before the court tomorrow, and you're up half the night playing math games!?"

Sheepishly he held out his hands. "It's . . . fun. I can't help myself. Besides, mathematics is important."

Fifty-three-year-old Pierre de Fermat was a lawyer and acted as king's council (or legal advisor) to the local parliament and court of Toulouse, France. While he was both competent and efficient at his job, he put neither enough time nor energy into it to measurably advance his career. Time and energy he saved for his two passions: his family and mathematics. Now that two of their three children were grown and out of the house, Fermat's thoughts and energies turned more and more to his hobby, his toy, his joy—mathematics.

Still, he provided well for his family—a comfortable living, a roomy, two-story house in a fashionable section of Toulouse—and he certainly couldn't be accused of spending all his time in his law office at work.

Now that it was obvious he'd been caught, Fermat lifted the law book and spread out the letters to show his wife. "I'm worried about Pascal."

"Is he sick? In danger?"

"No, no, Louise. I'm worried that he'll develop a working theory on predicting the probability of winning gambling games before I do."

From *Marvels of Math.* © 1998 Kendall Haven. Teacher Ideas Press. (800) 237-6124.

"But you don't gamble."

"It's a grand *math* puzzle. And it's about more than just the probability of winning at gambling. It's about discovering a whole theory of numbers and the rules that describe how they operate."

Louise slowly shook her head. "You're hopeless, Pierre. You spend all your free time on mathematics and don't even publish any of your discoveries."

Fermat's face wrinkled in disgust. "Writing and documenting what I've already done would be an utter bore. The joy is in the hunt, the race, the safari into the unknown, unraveling an age-old mystery."

Still shaking her head, Louise turned back toward bed, holding her candle in front of her. "Come to bed and get some sleep, or the 'mystery' will be how you'll stay awake in court tomorrow."

Fermat signed and pushed back from the desk. "Of course you're right, my dear." Half-standing he paused. "I still worry about Pascal, though. If only I could put my thoughts in some order . . ."

Again he chuckled. "I suppose my frustration with probability theory is why I'm so cruel to poor de Bessy, and give him the hardest problems I can construct."

In full lawyer robes the next afternoon, Fermat sat at his counselor's table in court, his shoulder length hair parted in the middle and flowing down over the stiff, high collar of his garb. Opposing lawyers droned on about their client's needs, morals, and their individual interpretations of justice and the facts.

With part of his mind Fermat was thinking about probability theory. With another part, he idly kept score of how many solid legal points each lawyer made. It struck Fermat that this was much like gambling. Here he had two opposing players of equal skill, the lawyers, each trying to make (or score) points with the judge. The question was how many points had each player scored?

No. Fermat realized the *real* question was how many more did they need to score to *win*? Was this the approach he needed to construct a probability theory?

From *Marvels of Math.* © 1998 Kendall Haven. Teacher Ideas Press. (800) 237-6124.

He was so engrossed with this new concept, Fermat almost missed hearing the judge refer a question to him for legal interpretation. As his portion of the trial ended, Fermat neither stayed to hear the verdict (as was the custom), nor returned to his office to work on opinions and briefs he needed to submit to Parliament.

Fermat raced to his home study where he worked on math problems. The question still roared in his mind, could he use the number of points each player still *needed* as a basis for predicting the probability of their victory?

He started with the simplest of all cases—when each of two players ("A" and "B") needed one more point to win. Here "one point" meant either winning the next flip of a coin, or the next roll of the dice. The contest would be decided with the next point.

The gamblers Fermat knew all said that the odds of each player's winning were even. Even odds seemed reasonable to Fermat. But were they correct? There were two ways that point could go, player A could win it, or player B could. One way gave A the win; The other gave B the win. With one way for each to win, the probability of each player winning was even. One point needed, two possibilities, even odds.

But what if A and B each needed *two* points to win? Would the probability still be even? That's what the gamblers all said. But were they right?

Fermat used the same approach to decide. The game would be decided within the next three points (each player could win one point without winning the match). How many possible ways could three points go? Fermat counted eight. All three points (or flips of a coin) could go to A. (Fermat wrote this as AAA). The first two could go to A and the third to B. (Fermat wrote this as AAB.) The other six possibilities were: ABA, BAA, ABB, BAB, BBA, and BBB.

If any of these possible combinations of points gave at least two points to A, then A would win. If at least two points went to B, B would win. Fermat counted the combinations and found four of the eight awarded two points to A, and four gave them to B. Two points needed, eight possible outcomes, again even odds of each player winning. The gamblers were correct.

Fermat set down his quill pen and nodded with satisfaction. These results matched what every gambler and player had observed and believed to be true.

From *Marvels of Math*. © 1998 Kendall Haven. Teacher Ideas Press. (800) 237-6124.

But would the system work when the situation was neither even, nor quite so obvious? What if A needed only 1 point to win but B needed 2? Intuition said the odds should be 2 to 1 in favor of A, the ratio of the number of points each player needed. Those were the odds gamblers used to determine their bets. But would that probability of winning be correct?

First, how many points (flips or rolls of the dice) must be played to guarantee a winner? Two. (B could win one point without deciding a winner. So within two points the game would be decided.)

Now, how many possible combinations were there for the two points, knowing each point could go to either A or B? Fermat counted four possible combinations. The first point could go to A and the second to B (AB), both could go to A (AA), both could go to B (BB), or the first could go to B and the second to A (BA).

Fermat rubbed his hand together. His approach to probability seemed to be working. "Now, who wins the game?"

Three of the four possibilities gave A his one needed point, and only one gave B his needed two. So the real odds of A winning were 3 to 1, not the 2 to 1 intuition predicted! The gamblers' system for predicting odds was wrong. The *actual* odds more strongly favored the player needing only one point.

"Fascinating," Fermat murmured.

With a rush of joyous discovery, Fermat decided to test the situation where player A needed two points to win, and player B needed three points. A winner would be decided within four points, since A could win one and B could win two without deciding a winner.

Fermat counted sixteen possible combinations of four points. One by one he checked them to see how many would give A his needed two points. (He found 11.) How many would give B his needed three? (There were five.)

That meant that the actual probability of A winning was 11 to 5 (written 11:5), while B's probability of winning was 5:11. The gamblers were wrong. The actual probability of winning much more strongly favored the player needing fewer points to win. 11:5 meant that player A actually won 70 percent of the time, instead of the 60 percent the gamblers intuitive method predicted.

Fermat had found a method for accurately predicting probabilities.

From *Marvels of Math.* © 1998 Kendall Haven. Teacher Ideas Press. (800) 237-6124.

Now, could he generalize his results into a form that would be applicable for all situations?

Fermat's wife came home. "How'd your case go, Pierre?"

From his desk he called, "I think I'm on to something!"

At his study door, she answered, "You sound excited, so it must be math again."

"I think I have the beginnings of a probability theory—in time to beat Pascal!"

"Congratulations. But how did your trial go?"

A wide smirk spread across Fermat's face as he turned to his wife. "To celebrate discovering a probability theory, I think I'll send an even *harder* problem to torment de Bessy. I know just the one. While reading a translation of Bachet's math book *Diophantus* a glorious theorem and proof occurred to me. He'll never figure it out!"

Fermat scanned his bookshelves, letting his fingers trail across the titles. "Ah, here it is."

"But what happened with the trial?"

Sheepishly Fermat shrugged. "I was so excited about probability theory, I didn't stay to find out."

∼∾ ∼∾ ∼∾

Pierre de Fermat may truly be called the "prince of amateur mathematicians." Many view him as the greatest mathematician of the seventeenth century. He made major contributions to analytical geometry, differential and integral calculus, and to probability and number theory.

But the famous story of Pierre de Fermat is not about probability. He *is* the father of modern probability and number theory. He *was* the first to devise a system for accurately predicting probability. This theory was his most important contribution to mathematics.

But if you mention Fermat's name to any mathematician, they will not think of probability. They will think of the mystery of Fermat's Last Theorem.

From *Marvels of Math*. © 1998 Kendall Haven. Teacher Ideas Press. (800) 237-6124.

The problem with Fermat was that he didn't publish, or even write down any of his work. He'd get an idea and scrawl it in the margin of the book he was reading. Thirty years after his death friends gathered all of the notes Fermat wrote in the margins of the many texts he had read and published them. The book included many important theorems on number theory, but Fermat had never written down any of the proofs! His notes would simply say that he had found one.

Mathematicians have spent centuries trying to duplicate Fermat's missing proofs and establish whether Fermat's many theorems were true or not. None have ever been proved false. Of the two problems Fermat sent to de Bessy that are mentioned in this story, the first was proved true a century later by LaGrange.

The second, called "Fermat's Last Theorem," has been the most famous math challenge on Earth for three centuries. The German Academy of Sciences offered a prize of 100,000 marks to anyone who could prove or disprove Fermat's Last Theorem. The prize went unclaimed.

In 1993, Princeton mathematician Andrew Wiles offered the world's first proof of this theorem. While the math world holds its breath, mathematicians are still analyzing Wiles' work to see if it contains any flaws. Whether Fermat's Last has finally been proved, is still another story.

Follow-on Questions and Activities to Explore

1. For the last probability problem listed in this story (A needs 2 points to win, B needs 3), list the 16 possible combinations of points. (An "A" means that player A wins that point. "B" means that player B wins that point.)

   Answer:
AAAA	AAAB	AABA	ABAA
BAAA	AABB	ABAB	BAAB
ABBA	BABA	BBAA	ABBB
BABB	BBAB	BBBA	BBBB

2. For which of these combinations would you really only have to play two points? For which ones would you really play only three points? For which combinations would you have to play all four points?

   Answer: In four combinations (1/4 of the total) the first two points go to A. So A would win without having to play any more points. The match is decided in two points. In six combinations (3/8 of the total) *either* two of the first three points go to A, or all of the first three go to B. Either way, the match is decided in three points. In the remaining six combinations (3/8 of the total) all four points must be played before a winner is decided.

3. Fermat's probability theory assumes that player A and player B have equal chances to win each point. He only worried about the odds of each player winning enough points to win the match. What would happen to your answer to question 1 if the coin being flipped to determine each point were weighted so that it came up heads (player B gets the point) twice as often as tails (where player A gets the point)? What would happen if the players were rolling a die, and player A got the point only if the die came up with a 1 or a 2, and player B got the point if it came up a 3, 4, 5, or 6?

   Answer: Even this simple change makes the probability very difficult to calculate using Fermat's method. If you were to write out all the new possible outcomes, you would increase from 16 to over 1200! Intuitively you know that player B now has a much higher probability of winning. But now it would be difficult to decide the exact likelihood of each player winning. Probability has become a very complex mathematical science and has developed many of its own mathematical concepts, theorems, and techniques that enable mathematicians to calculate probabilities much more complex than this problem.

Smaller
Makes Bigger

The Invention of Calculus
by Isaac Newton in 1666

At a Glance

Mathematicians develop new mathematical concepts and techniques to solve problems and more accurately describe observable phenomena in the world. Others search for ways to usefully apply them to solve new problems. A good example is surreal numbers, invented in 1992 as a way to count beyond infinity and describe the infinitesimally small. Scientists are still struggling to assess the potential and usefulness of this powerful new tool.

But more often, new mathematical concepts arise in direct response to a pressing need. Problems exist that can't be solved using existing numerical methods. So new numbers and methods are created.

Imaginary numbers are a good example. Solutions to higher order algebraic problems often created answers like $x^2 = -4$. That was an impossible answer. There was no number which, when multiplied by itself, produced a negative number. ($-1 \times -1 = +1$.) The equations couldn't be solved until a clever Italian mathematician invented imaginary numbers.

It was this type of problem that tormented English scientist Isaac Newton in the mid-1660s. He had discovered the forces that control how the moon revolves around the Earth, and how the Earth revolves around the sun. He had uncovered his laws of motion, which are still the basis for much of our scientific and engineering work.

But he had a problem. Available mathematics of the day would not allow him to adequately describe and calculate these forces and the complex motion of the moon and planets. He could identify and understand the forces. He could define them. He knew how they interacted to produce the motion of the moon and planets. But he couldn't calculate them.

He needed a new mathematical concept to allow him to solve this new kind of problem. That is when and why he created calculus.

Terms to Know

Understanding the following mathematical terms will help you understand and appreciate this story.

1. **Calculus.** Calculus is a specific kind of mathematics, as are arithmetic, algebra, geometry, and trigonometry. That is, calculus uses concepts and approaches to solving problems that are unique to calculus. Calculus is generally used for difficult problems that either cannot be solved algebraically, or are very difficult to solve algebraically.

    The key to calculus is that it breaks a problem up into an infinite number of infinitesimally small segments. Isaac Newton first devised a way to easily handle such a vast number of segments by creating a new mathematical technique called integration. Differentiation (the opposite of integration) and integration are the two basic processes of calculus.

2. **Velocity.** Velocity is a measure of speed, or how fast something moves. Car velocity, for example, we measure in miles per hour. The Earth's tectonic plates move a fraction of an inch per year. Velocity is always measured as some distance moved in a certain amount of time.

3. **Acceleration.** Acceleration is a measure of changes in velocity. Commonly we say something is either speeding up, or slowing down. Speeding up is positive acceleration. Slowing down is negative acceleration, or deceleration. Acceleration is measured as a change in velocity over a certain amount of time. If a car accelerated from zero to 10 miles per hour in one second, we say that its acceleration was ten miles per hour per second.

4. **Linear.** Linear means in a straight line. Equations where nothing is raised to a power (other than 1) will graph as straight lines. Equations with terms raised to higher powers and equations with periodic functions all graph as curved lines.

5. **Equation.** An equation is the general form used to solve algebraic problems. In an equation two mathematical quantities, or terms, are set equal to each other. The equal sign (=) is used to connect the two terms.

    $x = 3a + 2b$ is an equation. It means that the quantity x (whatever that is) is exactly equal to three times whatever a represents plus three times whatever b represents. It is essential to know what is equal to what in solving an algebraic equation.

6. **Infinite.** Infinite means "as large as infinity," or "stretching to infinity." In mathematical terms, infinity is not a number. It is a term to mean "beyond all known numbers," or "bigger than we can count or measure." The mathematical symbol for infinity is "∞."

7. **Infinitesimal.** The opposite of infinity is infinitesimal, meaning "so small that we can't measure or count it." Mathematically, infinitesimal is expressed as one divided by infinity, or "$1/\infty$."

Smaller Makes Bigger

"You're sitting out here *again*, Uncle Isaac?"

Unseen bees buzzed contentedly from tree to tree and bush to bush. Butterflies flitted back and forth above rolling lawns dotted with tufts of flowers. It was a lovely country English garden beginning again to shine in all its splendor as rumbling clouds gave way to ever-widening patches of brilliant blue.

"I like it out here, Josh. It's quiet and I can think."

"But you'll get all *wet* 'cause it rained this morning!"

Twenty-three-year-old math and science teacher Isaac Newton glanced down at the growing dark ring of wet on his breeches and top coat. "I suppose I am." With fair complexion, slight, frail-looking build, and pale, stringy blond hair, he looked much younger than his years. "I'm out here because I have a problem to think about."

"*Again*?! Don't you ever want to play?" Isaac's eight-year-old nephew Joshua Marsh was an energetic bundle of thick brown hair and questions. "Mother and her friends in the parlor said you don't know how to have fun. But I said you do *so*. You'd just rather think. Isn't that right?"

Isaac chuckled and reached out to ruffle his nephew's hair. "Right now all I can think about is a big problem I can't solve."

The year was 1666. England lay in the terrible grip of the plague, a deadly disease. Universities were closed and important professors, like Isaac Newton, had fled to country estates to escape the dreaded disease that spread through English cities. Newton was stuck at his sister's isolated estate in Woolsthorpe.

Joshua plopped into the wet grass next to his uncle, sounding more like an uncle plopping into the grass to help a struggling nephew. "Whatcha thinkin' 'bout this time, Uncle Isaac?"

"The moon."

From *Marvels of Math*. © 1998 Kendall Haven. Teacher Ideas Press. (800) 237-6124.

"*Again*?! You already figured out the moon has an invisible gravity string that holds it to the earth."

"Very good," laughed Isaac. "You remember."

Joshua nodded. "I *knew* you knew how to laugh and have fun."

"I may *know* the forces that make the moon move as it does, Josh. But . . ." Isaac sighed and his face turned as dark as the morning storm clouds. "But now I can't *describe* the effect of those forces."

"Can you 'scribe 'em to me?"

"I have to *mathematically* describe the effect of each force, and our system of algebraic equations is too limited. Algebra allows me to look at only one moment in time, like a painting."

Joshua's face beamed. "I like painting!"

"Like algebra, a painting of a runner shows one moment in time, but not how fast he's running, or what his strides are like, or how he's turning. But those are the terms I need to calculate."

Uncle Isaac's explanation didn't help. Joshua's face wrinkled up in confusion. "You want to paint a picture of a runner on the moon?"

"A mathematical picture of forces, Josh," Newton continued, mostly talking to himself. "Force creates motion . . ."

"What's a force?"

"A push or a pull, Josh. But . . ."

"What's a *motion*, Uncle Isaac?"

Newton sighed. "Motion is movement."

"Oh. So when you push something it moves?"

"Yes, Josh. But . . ."

"That's not hard math. Even I know *that*."

Newton sighed and shook his head as shafts of strong summer light poured down into the garden, and as fierce-looking clouds gathered along the western horizon. "Force *changes* motion. *That's* the problem."

Newton was instantly lost deep in the world of his thoughts, blocking out the outside world. "Algebra can describe a steady motion, but it won't describe *change* in motion. How do I mathematically combine position, velocity, and changing motion, or acceleration?"

"What's an axle-eration, Uncle Isaac?"

Newton jumped, startled by the question as if, in his thought, he had forgotten his nephew was there. "Acceleration, Josh. It's . . ." Newton paused, thinking of how to describe the concept. "See those two apple trees, Josh?"

The boy nodded.

"Run over there, and run around them a few times."

"Oh, boy! A game." Joshua took off like a shot, his shoes slipping in the wet grass.

Newton cupped his hands and called, "Run faster, Josh! Now slow down. Now faster again."

In an all-out sprint, Joshua slipped on a tight turn and tumbled across the grass. He sat up, panting.

"Speeding up and slowing down—that's acceleration."

Trying to wipe the wet off his hands, face, and clothes, Joshua said, "Next time, just tell me."

"You always learn better when you *do* something."

Joshua frowned. "Then next time just teach me a little bit of axle-eration. I'm tired."

Newton's laugh faded as the potential of Joshua's words sank in. "A little part, a smaller part . . . a *very* small part of a curve almost *looks* like a straight line. A very small piece of an acceleration curve *looks* as straight as linear velocity. . . . The problem with algebra is that it looks at big pieces of complex systems and can't adequately describe them. Maybe if I looked at very small pieces I can solve my problem."

A rumble of distant thunder made Newton glance up. "We better head in, Josh. It's going to rain again."

From *Marvels of Math.* © 1998 Kendall Haven. Teacher Ideas Press. (800) 237-6124.

"Can we play with my mom and the other guests then?"

Newton shook his head. "You've given me a new idea to think about, Josh."

The boy straightened with a new sense of pride. "I gave *you* an idea?" His small fists rose to his hips. "Well?"

"Well, *what*, Josh? It's starting to sprinkle."

"Say, 'thank you.' Mother says you should always say 'thank you' when someone gives you something."

Newton laughed as the drops began to splat thick and hard around them. "Thank you for your idea, Josh. I'll let you know if it works."

Rain pelted the gabled roof of the estate. Smoke billowed up chimneys from fires trying to hold back the damp chill. Joshua, his mother, and other guests talked, laughed, and played music and parlor games. Isaac Newton paced in his upstairs room as streams of rainwater flowed down the window panes.

"Break the analysis into small pieces. . . . Into *which* small pieces? . . . Pieces of *what*? How small can I make the pieces? What does breaking an equation up this way allow me to do that I cannot do now?"

Hands clasped behind his back, oblivious to the raucous downstairs noise or the pounding of rain, Newton tumbled the ideas over and over in his mind, debating both sides of each concept. "Small pieces. . . . If I break a problem into a very large number of very small increments, I will be able to use existing algebra to approximate the motion of the moon, the forces that pull it, and the acceleration of its motion into an orbit around the sun. But I need *exact* solutions, not approximations. If I made the increments very small, it would produce a very good approximation. But it would still be only an approximation! What if I made the increments *infinitesimally* small? Then I'd have an infinitely large number of them to add up. But the error would also be infinitesimally small, so small that, in effect, I would have an exact solution."

The idea rumbled louder than outside thunder through Newton's head. It tingled like a lightning strike through his body. Using algebraic concepts to sum the results of an infinitely large number of infinitesimally small intervals would produce an exact solution!

But how to do it?

Out loud, Newton said to himself as he hurried to his overflowing bookshelves, "Something like this has been tried before . . ."

Early that evening, Joshua found his uncle at his desk, surrounded by stacks of open books on the ancient Greeks, Archimedes, Galileo, Kepler, Cardano, Fermat, and Huygens. "Whatcha doin?" Joshua's head poked around the partly opened study door.

"Math."

"Na uh. You're still reading. You were reading when I brought you supper an hour ago."

Newton glanced at the plate of now cold food with surprise. "Mercy me. I forgot all about it! I've been too excited reading about what past mathematicians discovered and attempted."

Joshua shuffled in and leaned both elbows on his uncle's desk. "Doesn't sound very exciting."

"On the contrary, Josh. It's *thrilling*. Many of these past mathematicians thought about studying infinitely small increments. But they all lacked real problems that needed this analysis to focus their efforts. Luckily, I have that with my problem of describing the changing acceleration of the moon around the earth in accordance with my law of motion (F=ma, or force equals mass times acceleration). Past mathematicians also lacked an idea for how to make infinitesimal analysis work in a practical sense."

"What's an infinitesimal?"

"I'll show you, Josh. Tear that piece of paper in half. Now tear that in half again. Is your piece smaller?"

"Sure, Uncle Isaac. That's easy."

From *Marvels of Math*. © 1998 Kendall Haven. Teacher Ideas Press. (800) 237-6124.

"But is it *infinitesimally* small?"

Joshua shrugged. "I don't know what . . ."

"No, it is not," interrupted Newton. "Not even close. Tear it in half again. And again. And again. And again. And again."

"It's getting *tiny* now, Uncle Isaac." Joshua stared at the small scrap pinched between his finger tips.

"But is it infinitesimal?"

Joshua confidently nodded. "Probably is. It's almost too small to hold."

"Not even close," Newton replied. "Tear it in half five more times."

"*Five* more!" gasped Joshua.

"Then ten more times after that."

"I couldn't even see it!"

"Pretend you could. Then tear it in half a thousand more times, and a thousand-thousand more after that."

Joshua seemed truly alarmed. "But it'd be *nothing* by then!"

Newton smiled, "And that's what infinitesimal is. Not nothing, but smaller than you could ever measure."

Joshua pouted, "You could have just *told* me. Now I've made a big mess of ripped-up paper."

"You learn better when you . . ."

"I know," interrupted Joshua. "I learn better when I *do* something. Do I have to clean up the mess now?"

Isaac Newton reached out and lovingly mussed his nephew's hair. "Thank you for offering, Josh. That would be nice. And be thankful you weren't able to rip the paper into infinitesimally small pieces. Think of how many you'd have to pick up then. That's how many pieces I have to mathematically add up when I break a problem into infinitely small pieces."

"It'll probably take you *days* to add 'em all up, Uncle Isaac!"

Newton laughed. "It only takes a few moments, Josh. What I have discovered is a new kind of mathematics, a new way to simplify and solve equations that's just perfect for my particular problem."

On his hands and knees, Joshua muttered, "I hope your mathematics works better on problems than this broom does on tiny pieces of paper."

And so, the idea of calculus was born. Newton's ideas created what we call integration, or integral calculus. Through integration Newton found mathematical ways to do quickly what would have otherwise taken countless lifetimes—add up an infinite number of infinitely small increments that make up a problem.

Newton was then able to show that differentiation, another similar process was really part of his new calculus. Calculus created a whole new way to solve problems too complex for algebra to handle. Without Newton's calculus, modern physics, chemistry, oceanography, astronomy, and most other quantitative sciences could never have been developed.

Isaac Newton, called by many the greatest mathematician in all history, also discovered the three great laws of motion which dictated how physics, engineering, and astronomy would develop for over two hundred years. Besides his two great discoveries, Newton made major contributions to number series, optics, and other areas of general mathematics.

When Newton wrote his discoveries of calculus and the laws of motion into a book, titled *Principia*, he wrote eighteen hours a day, seven days a week, for almost two years, often never making it out of bed or his nightclothes. But who taught all the classes Newton skipped while writing *Principia*, is another story.

Follow-on Question and Activity to Explore

To make his answer more accurate Isaac Newton broke his problem into smaller and smaller parts until each part was infinitesimally small and he had an infinite number of parts to add up. Without going to such extremes you can see how an answer grows more accurate as you break the problem into smaller pieces.

Here is a simple demonstration.

1. Draw a large circle on a piece of paper. If you didn't know the formula for the area of a circle, how would you figure out how big it was? That is, how much area lay inside the circle. Use Newton's general approach. Fit shapes you *do* know (let's start with a square) inside the circle and see how your answer improves as you decrease the size of each part.

2. Draw (inscribe) a square inside your circle so that the corners just touch the circle. (See figure, p. 103.) You could easily find the area of this square. But you can see that the square isn't quite the same size as the circle.

3. Now make each side of the square smaller so that you will have more sides. How? Inscribe an octagon (eight-sided shape) inside the circle so that its corners just touch the circle. (Hint: As shown in figure on p. 103, the easiest way to do this is to draw a line from the center of the circle that exactly cuts in half each angle formed by the lines from the center out to the corners of the square.)

4. Connect all eight points to form an octagon. Can you see that, by making each segment smaller and by having more of them, you better approximate the shape and area of the circle?

5. Now cut each side of the octagon in half to form a sixteen-sided object. Is this coming very close to looking like your circle?

Answer: Compare your answer with those of other students and discuss as a class.

Estimating area by creating smaller and smaller segments.

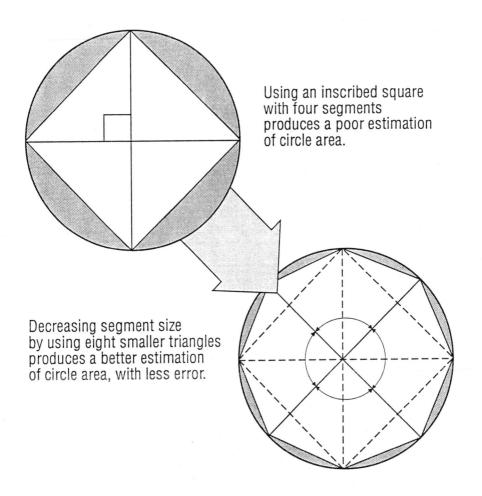

Using an inscribed square
with four segments
produces a poor estimation
of circle area.

Decreasing segment size
by using eight smaller triangles
produces a better estimation
of circle area, with less error.

A Bridge to Math

The Invention of Topology
by Leonhard Euler in 1736

At a Glance

Leonhard Euler was the most prolific mathematician in all history, publishing over 500 books and papers, for an average of over 800 pages a year. More importantly, Euler created more standardized notation than any other individual in the history of math. Only two other persons created two mathematical notations we still use. No one other than Euler ever created more than two. His *seven* include π, e, Σ, log x, sin x, cos x, and f(x). Euler advanced our understanding of the moon's motion, infinite series, the theory of numbers, and he created a new branch of geometry called topology. This is the story of that creation.

Terms to Know

Understanding the following mathematical terms will help you understand and appreciate this story.

1. **Series and Infinite Series.** A series is any number of similar things occurring one after the other in some pattern. 1, 2, 3, 4 . . . is a series. So is 2, 4, 6, 8 . . . and 2, 4, 16, 256 . . . . So is (x + 2), (x² + 4x + 4), (x⁴ + 8x³ + 24x² + 22x + 16). . . . Series are often expressed as equations, as in x = 1 - 2 + 3 - 4 + 5 - 6 + 7 . . .

    An infinite series is a series that goes on forever. All of the series listed above are infinite series because the terms could go on forever following the same pattern. There are two different symbols that may be used to indicate that a series is an infinite series. The first is a ". . ." following the last term listed in the series. The ". . ." may be listed any time after the nature of the pattern of the series has been established. The other symbol is an "n" in place of the last term, as in x = 1 + 2 - 3 + 4 - 5 + n. Here the "n" indicates that the series goes on for some arbitrary number of terms (n).

2. **Convergent.** A series is convergent if its value grows closer and closer to a specific point or value. The motion of a swinging door is an example of a physical convergent series. First the door swings out. Then it swings back in, but not as far. Then it swings back out—but again, not as far. Then back in, then back out, always coming closer and closer to a final value in the exact middle.

$x = 1/2 + 1/3 + 1/4 + 1/5 + 1/6 \ldots$ is also a convergent series. Each new term in the series grows smaller and smaller so that the value for the whole series approaches a single, fixed value.

3. **Divergent.** Divergent series are the opposite of convergent series. If a series of numbers is divergent, it will never come closer and closer to a fixed, single value. Instead, a divergent series grows toward plus or minus infinity. All divergent series are infinite series.

$x = 1 + 2 + 3 + 4 + 5 + 6 \ldots$ is a simple divergent series.

4. **Topology.** Topology is one kind of geometric study. Topology is not concerned with magnitudes, amounts, or with sizes, but only with position and its properties. Topology does not involve measurement or calculation. It studies how elements are placed, or arrayed, and how that placement determines other properties.

This story is about a topology problem. Notice that, in determining whether or not the mayor's parade may be held, Euler never calculates anything about the bridges or land masses (size, length, height, etc.). It is only their relative position he considers.

5. **Reciprocal.** In math, the reciprocal of a number is 1 divided by that number. The reciprocal of 3 is 1/3. The reciprocal of 12.5 is 1/12.5. The reciprocal of 1/4 is 4.

By definition, the reciprocal of a number is that number which, when multiplied by the original number equals unity (1). A number times its reciprocal always equals one.

A Bridge to Math

"How can I concentrate in here? It's freezing!" The frail professor blew into his cupped hands. "Dimitri, please get more wood. Brains that are freezing can't concentrate on my lectures and solve math problems."

"But I fetched wood last time, Professor Euler (OI-ler)."

"And you'll fetch wood every time I catch you napping in class, Dimitri." With a smug chuckle Professor Euler added, "Didn't think I'd catch you crouching in the back, did you?"

Blond, muscular, nineteen-year-old Dimitri pushed back his chair and shuffled toward the door with a resigned huff. Passing the desk of a friend, he whispered, "How can a blind professor know every time I close my eyes?"

"I have lost my sight, but not my hearing, Dimitri." Again Euler chuckled. Twenty-nine years old, and blind for the past three years, Leonhard Euler delighted in catching students who thought they could take advantage of his disability. "And don't be long, Dimitri. I know that the wood pile is just outside the back door of this building."

"That one's empty, Professor. It's been a long winter."

"Every winter in St. Petersburg, Russia is longer and colder than the last," added Euler, again blowing on his fingers. "Why should this winter of 1736 be any different?"

Euler's classroom at the St. Petersburg Academy (or University) was sparse, even though he was now chair of the math department. Still, it was little more than a plain, rectangular wooden box with few windows, years of wax polished onto the floor, creaky floorboards, tiny desks for the forty burly students, flickering, smoky gas lamps, and only one small stove for heat.

Now, in late March of 1736, St. Petersburg was buried in a deep, winter blanket of snow that would not make way for flowery spring until June.

Professor Euler turned back to his bundled students. "We were discussing infinite series, were we not, before winter cold interrupted our thoughts?"

Euler sat in a straight-back chair next to a long table as he taught, his thin arms resting in his lap, as if they were too frail to lift themselves, though they were really stout enough to lift and toss his four young children. His face could be described as nothing but plain and unnoteworthy except for the warm and mischievous smile that lingered on his lips far more than it was absent.

Dimitri kicked open the door and staggered in, panting, with an armful of wood.

Euler nodded. "With wood comes warmth. With warmth comes clarity. Thank you, Dimitri. And try to stay awake while we talk about convergent and divergent infinite series."

The class chuckled. Dimitri sank, red-faced, into his seat.

Euler continued. "We'll start with the following simple series. Say I want to know the sum of the following infinite series: $x = 1 - 2 + 3 - 4 + 5 - 6 + n$. Peter, please write it on the board for all to see."

As brown-haired Peter's chalk scratched out the equation, Euler continued. "Is this convergent or divergent? Hands. Who knows?"

"It's a convergent series," said one boy in the back. "No matter how big the numbers get, the series adds up to 0. I mean, the sum of the series for some number of terms, n, plus the sum for n + 1 terms equals 0. So it is always trying to converge to 0."

"Does anyone disagree?" asked the professor.

"I think it's divergent," offered Dimitri. "The individual terms increase forever until they reach to infinity. That makes it divergent rather than convergent."

Euler smiled and rubbed his hands. "Good. Argument on both sides. But only one can be right. We must discuss and decide. I think we should start by comparing that first series to its reciprocal: $x = 1/1 - 1/2 + 1/3 - 1/4 + 1/5 - 1/6 + 1/n$. Peter write it for the class if you would, please."

Euler waited until the chalk scrapings stopped. "Dimitri. Is *this* equation convergent or divergent?"

Dimitri hesitated, studying the equation, scanning through old notes for comparisons. "Definitely convergent, professor."

"Why?"

"Each new term in the series grows smaller, decreasing toward 0. So the series converges closer and closer to a single value for x."

Euler's fists raised over his head. "Very good Dimitri. Exactly right. Now back to the first equation."

Again the students' focus on mathematics was interrupted, this time by a discussion, or argument, growing louder every moment in the office next door. Classroom debate and conversation ceased. All eyes stared at the connecting door as the voices rose to high-pitched screaming on the other side.

Abruptly the shouting stopped. Ominous quiet filled the room. The connecting door cracked open and then timidly creaked back. Her full floor-length skirt swishing with each step, Madam Brovinski, the Math Department secretary, crept into the room. Her reddened face was cocked down so she wouldn't have to look at the students she disrupted with this unprecedented intrusion.

"Please excuse my interruption, Professor Euler, but there's a German man . . ."

From the other room a booming voice broke over hers, "Herr Gunterling, the Grand Mayor of Königsberg!"

Madam Brovinski's face hardened. Her eyebrows narrowed. She continued in a lower voice. "A *rude* German man who says he must see you right away concerning a math problem."

Euler held up one hand. "Tell him to see a German mathematician."

"He has, sir—all of them. No one can solve his problem. And he's running out of time."

"*None* of them can solve it?" repeated Euler, his face brightening.

"None, sir."

"I have tried them all," shouted the mayor. "You are the last hope for the Königsberg parade."

Euler (who had been born in Switzerland and had studied in Germany before moving to the University in St. Petersburg) turned back to face his class, grinning like a child about to open a giant Christmas present box. "Dare we pass up this opportunity to point out the deficiencies of every living German mathematician?"

The Russian students laughed.

Euler motioned to Madam Brovinski. "Bring in the good mayor. We will hear his problem."

The rotund mayor swept in wearing a great bear-skin coat. His face was a sea of circles—round eyes, round, pudgy nose, bright round cheeks, round chin. With a brief nod toward the students, he swept Euler's math books aside and unfurled a large map of Königsberg across the table. "As you can see . . ."

The words caught in the mayor's throat as he glanced down and realized Euler was blind. His face reddened. "Excuse me, Professor Euler. I had no idea."

Euler's playful smile spread across his lips. "Just state your problem, Herr Mayor. I have a good mind for holding and concentrating on mathematics."

"*Good?*" whispered one of the students. "He can solve whole complex equations in his head that I can barely figure out on paper."

Now the mayor tried to describe the situation for Euler. "Two rivers meet in Königsberg to form the mighty River Pregel. Right where they meet, the River Pregel's channel splits around a large island that is the heart of old Königsberg. Königsberg is a city of seven bridges—two from the south shore of the river to the old city island, two from the north shore to the old city island, and one each from the peninsula between the two rivers to the south shore, the north shore, and the old city island."

Euler held up a hand to interrupt. "I can visualize your city. Peter, please draw it on the board so everyone can see. What is your math problem Herr Mayor?"

"In one month Königsberg will hold its thousand-year celebration. We'll have a grand parade, which, by legend, must cross every bridge in Königsberg, but may only cross them once. No one can design a parade route that crosses each bridge once and once only. Nor can they tell me if it is even possible."

Euler nodded. "There, class, is our problem. What do you think? Is it possible?"

One student shrugged. "They have plenty of bridges. It's bound to be possible in some way."

"I've already tried several routes," said another. "And none of them work. I say it's impossible."

"We need proof!" bellowed Euler. "Not guesses. If it is impossible, is it because of the number of bridges, or the number of land masses, or both? We need to present a general solution that will answer the question for *any* number of bridges and *any* number of land masses."

Professor Euler sat motionless for some time, as his students knew, his mind was laying out and solving the entire problem. Finally Euler sucked in a great breath and smiled. "I see the fundamental elements of your problem, Herr Mayor. Let my secretary know where you are staying in St. Petersburg. I'll send word as soon as a solution is ready."

"But you *can* solve it?" asked the mayor.

"I certainly don't see why not. But if you will excuse me, today we are discussing infinite series."

Three days later Mayor Gunterling was summoned to Euler's classroom. "The problem is solved," announced Euler. "You may tell your German mathematicians that they may always count on Russia when they get stuck."

Again the students laughed. The mayor's face reddened.

"The solution comes from looking not at bridges, but at land masses," continued Euler. "Let's label your four land masses 'A' for the island, 'B' for the south shore, 'C' for the peninsula, and 'D' for the north shore."

Peter dutifully labeled the areas on the board.

"Now a trip from A to B over any bridge is noted as AB. (One bridge crossed, two letters written.) If we continue to C we note the trip as ABC. (Two bridges crossed, three letters written.)"

Euler paused and reached for the mayor's arm. "Are you with me so far?"

"Yes. But can we hold our parade?"

Euler smiled and patted the mayor's arm. "All in good time. First the math, then the parade. So we see that a trip over any number of bridges, say 'n' bridges, will require us to touch n+1 land masses.

"We may follow the same logic for each land mass. If a single land mass, say 'A' is touched by an even number of bridges, say 2n (2n is always even no matter what value n holds), then A must be touched either n or n+1 times depending on whether you start somewhere else or on A."

"Can we hold our parade?!" demanded the mayor.

"Let me finish. Now if a land mass is touched by an *odd* number of bridges—call the number 2n+1, because no matter what 'n' is, 2n+1 is always odd—then that land mass must be touched *exactly* n+1 times to cross every bridge. It doesn't matter if you start on that land mass or off of it.

"Now we can begin to search for ways to touch each land mass the required number of times and still have seven bridge crossings and touch land masses a total of eight times."

"Can I schedule the parade!?!" bellowed the mayor.

"I will answer the mathematics question you asked," answered Euler in icy tones. "Then you decide if you can hold your parade. The key turns out to be the number of land masses that are touched by an odd number of bridges. If there are more than two of those, the answer is always no. If there are two or fewer, the answer is yes, so long as you start on one of those land masses."

"CAN I HOLD MY PARADE!?!" The mayor trembled with frustrated rage.

Euler slowly turned to face the mayor. "No."

Mayor Gunterling staggered back, thunderstruck. His voice suddenly small as a church mouse's. "No?"

"You have four land masses touched by an odd number of bridges. The parade is impossible unless you build a new bridge, or tear down one of the old ones."

Pale and trembling, the mayor swept his map off the table and stormed out.

From *Marvels of Math.* © 1998 Kendall Haven. Teacher Ideas Press. (800) 237-6124.

But by asking Euler to study the question, the mayor helped to create a new branch of mathematics, topology. Topology, a sub-branch of geometry, is not concerned with magnitudes, or with sizes, but only with position and its properties. Topology does not involve measurement or calculation. It studies how elements are placed, or arrayed, and how that placement determines other properties.

We now call topology "graph theory," and use it to solve complex relationship problems. But whether Königsberg ever got their parade, or whether Dimitri ever passed math class are each another story.

Follow-on Questions and Activities to Explore

1. Do you think Euler's topology principal works? Try it yourself and see with the following demonstration.

    Get a current map of New York City. Trace the outline of Manhattan Island, the Bronx, Queens and Brooklyn on Long Island, and the New Jersey shore of the Hudson River. Draw in all bridges that connect these four land masses going only as far north as the George Washington Bridge, and ignoring the Verrezano Narrows Bridge between Long Island and Staten Island. Count the Tri-borough Bridge as two bridges, one connecting the Bronx to Manhattan, and one connecting the Bronx to Long Island.

    How many bridges are there? How many bridges touch each land mass? Could you design a parade route to cross each bridge once and only once? Are your results consistent with what Euler's theory predicted?

    Answer: Yes, your results should be consistent with Euler. Only two land masses (New Jersey and the Bronx) have an odd number of bridges touching them so you'd have to start on one of those two places. If you do, you'll easily be able to draw out a number of possible parade routes. Of course, your feet would get real sore if you had to walk the whole route! So Euler's theory seems to be correct.

2. Add in the Verrazano Narrows Bridge. (Pretend that Staten Island is part of the New Jersey side of the Hudson River.) *Now* will your parade route work?

    Answer: Yes. There are still only two land masses with odd numbers of bridges—now Long Island and the Bronx. As long as you start in one of those two places, the route is still possible.

The Truth About "M. Le Blanc"

Sophie Germain's Start Toward Her Development of the Theory of Elasticity in 1794

At a Glance

Across Europe in the late eighteenth century women were viewed as frail, delicate creatures incapable of much understanding or mental concentration. In France it was commonly believed that if a woman tried to think too deeply it would make her faint, or more likely, make her physically sick.

No academic school would admit women because they had no need for, or use of, academic learning. A woman certainly couldn't get hired for a technical or skilled job. She certainly couldn't have a career.

The strongest bastion of this chauvinistic thinking was the famed French university, Ecole Normale. Women, even wives of professors, were not allowed to even *visit* the University, much less attend classes. A serious academic campus was no place for a woman.

Professor Joseph LaGrange, head of the university's math department, was a staunch supporter of the policy barring women on campus and from fields such as mathematics. Then in late 1794 LaGrange's beliefs were turned upside down as young Sophie Germain cracked open the door to women in math.

Terms to Know

Understanding the following mathematical terms will help you understand and appreciate this story.

1. **Differential.** Differential is a term used in calculus. A differential equation is one in which the derivative of an expression (one of the two main operations in calculus) is multiplied by a small increment in an unknown variable. It is not necessary to understand anything about calculus to understand this story. This brief explanation is included because the lead character, Sophie Germain, once refers to a differential transformation equation, a procedure developed by Joseph LaGrange for solving certain kinds of calculus problems.

The Truth About "M. Le Blanc"

Early December snows swirled bitter-cold down Paris walkways and alleys. The afternoon sky grew dark with coal soot from countless chimneys long before the sun set under lead-gray clouds. Five years after the fall of the Bastille and the start of the French Revolution in December 1794, the still somber mood in Paris matched this dreary sky. A few Christmas carolers half-heatedly wandered the streets. But their harmonies seemed swallowed up by the echoing dull thud of guillotine blades, still active in the larger Paris squares.

Every day, it seemed, Paris lives were forever changed. Heads were lost. Babies were born. Trials of the French Revolution were still held. Fortunes and property were seized. But no change during that December of 1794 affected the world of science more than the changes to eighteen-year-old Sophie Germain.

For five years Sophie had been cooped up in the family house on Rue St. Denis. Her parents feared for her safety outside. For five years she had stayed indoors with her dark, solemn eyes, her plain, honest face, and her quiet, dignified manner, and she read.

Luckily, Sophie loved to read, especially chemistry and math. But reading wasn't nearly enough. Sophie longed to hear the great scientists of her day, to ask them questions, to challenge their thinking.

But there was no place for a girl in the world of science. It was common knowledge in those days that women were incapable of grasping scientific and mathematical concepts. Such intense thought would only make them dizzy and faint, if not actually ill.

But at 5:15 AM one frigid morning, Sophie Germain's life began to change. That morning Sophie's father caught her studying at her desk again. Actually, he caught her asleep at her desk wrapped in a blanket from her bed, pen still held loosely in her right hand, ink frozen in her ink horn, equations he could not begin to understand scrawled across her slate.

Her father, Ambroise Germain, slammed his hand down onto Sophie's desk. She squealed in fright, bolted upright, and sprawled backwards off her chair onto the floor.

From *Marvels of Math.* © 1998 Kendall Haven. Teacher Ideas Press. (800) 237-6124.

Sophie's mother, Marie, wrung her hands and paced nervously near the door. Their breath seemed to freeze in the icy air. Shadows danced across their faces from the lone candle Ambroise held. "Why, daughter," he bellowed, "do you insist on disobeying the best wishes of your parents?!"

Even as Sophie groggily pulled herself from sleep, there was no hint of silly girlishness, fear, or anger on her face—just a deep seriousness and an unstoppable, unyielding dedication to her beliefs.

Sophie's father began to pace before her as she sat next to her fallen chair on the floor.

"I'm not opposed to your studying, Sophie. But if you must study, study something *useful* like music, Latin, or art."

"What could be more useful than math and chemistry, father."

"I mean for a *woman!*" he shouted and again slammed his fist on her desk so that her ink horn jumped and almost tipped over.

Her mother added pleadingly, "You're a girl, Sophie, delicate and frail by nature. This much thinking will certainly ruin your health. We just want what's best for you, dear."

Ambroise returned to his pacing. "First I took away the heater in your room to keep you from this ridiculous night studying. Then I locked up all your clothes, and then the candles so you'd have neither warmth nor light. Finally, I hid all paper and pens. Goodness knows where you steal these from!"

He picked up Sophie's slate and shook it at her. Then he paused and frowned at the equations. "And what is this gibberish?"

"It's one of Professor LaGrange's second order differential transformations, father."

Her mother's face looked as if she had just sucked on a bitter lemon. "A different *what*?!"

Ambroise scowled. "What sort of nonsense is a second—transformation?"

"It's an equation, father."

"I can see it's math. And never mind what it is," growled Ambroise. "It's a silly waste of time. *That's* what it is. Why do you do this to us, Sophie?"

From *Marvels of Math*. © 1998 Kendall Haven. Teacher Ideas Press. (800) 237-6124.

Sophie rose, slowly righted her chair, and sat, primly straightening her night gown. "Have you heard of Archimedes, father? You have? Good. Did you know that when the Romans invaded his city he was so engrossed in a geometry problem that he failed to respond to the Roman soldier's questions, and they killed him. How fascinating math must be to command such attention!" Then she added quietly, "Besides, I have to study."

"*Have* to? Why *have* to?" asked her father with raised eyebrows.

Sophie lowered her eyes to her desk. She was sure her father wouldn't like this part. "To keep up with my class," she answered softly.

"Class?! What class?" he demanded.

Now she proudly threw back her head and looked straight into her father's eyes. "Professor LaGrange's mathematics class at the University, Ecole Normale."

Ambroise shook his head and laughed. "Don't be silly, daughter. Girls are not allowed to even visit the University, much less attend classes."

"My friend, Gaston, loans me his class notes. I even submitted a paper this term."

"A famous professor at the University will never accept a paper from a girl," laughed her father.

Now Sophie smiled. "Yes he will, father. I didn't use my own name."

Sophie's mother wrung her hands and moaned. "If word gets out our daughter's studying math we'll be the laughingstock of Paris. Besides, it can't possibly be good for your health."

∾ ∾ ∾

At 2 PM, Professor Joseph LaGrange leaned casually back in his leather and oak desk chair. On the wide table before him were spread nearly eighty term papers. Fellow professor, Gaspard Monge, puffed on his pipe in a second overstuffed chair. The smoke curled up along book-lined walls to an ornate chandelier above. LaGrange picked up one of the papers and slid it across the table to Monge.

"I have selected the winning paper for this fall's term. This one. It's brilliant, insightful, and concise. But I don't recognize the name of this student, M. Le Blanc. Do you know him?"

From *Marvels of Math.* © 1998 Kendall Haven. Teacher Ideas Press. (800) 237-6124.

Gaspard stopped his smoking and looked thoughtfully up to the ceiling. "Le Blanc, Le Blanc. No. It doesn't ring a bell. Let me see the paper."

Gaspard Monge pulled reading spectacles from his breast pocket and scanned through M. Le Blanc's paper. "I see why you chose it. Extraordinary. Obviously a thoughtful and astute young man. Must have attended all your lectures to obtain such insight. Surprising, I don't recall his name."

LaGrange shrugged and straightened himself in his chair. "Well, no matter. I'm sure we'll recognize him at the award ceremony I've scheduled for tomorrow afternoon."

Gaspard nodded, rose, and stepped to the door. "Is your wife coming to the ceremony this year, Joseph?"

LaGrange looked shocked. "Certainly not! No woman has ever attended the award ceremony at the end of a term, and they never will. It would be most inappropriate. Besides mathematics just confuses a female. They are not capable of understanding such things."

∾ ∾ ∾

The next afternoon, just before 2 PM, Sophie Germain nervously tip-toed down the wide second floor hall to Professor LaGrange's office. Gaston prodded her from behind at every step to keep her from scurrying back home. The whole university was assembled in the auditorium one floor below to honor this term's mathematics winner, Monsieur Le Blanc.

Professor LaGrange anxiously opened the door to Sophie's light knock, calling, "Le Blanc? Is that you? You're . . ." The final words of the sentence hung frozen in his mouth as he opened the door and saw who stood before him. "And who, might I ask, are you?" he asked in icy tones.

Sophie curtsied. "I'm Sophie Germain."

With a sneer, LaGrange gazed past her down the hallway, then at his pocket watch. "Yes, I'm sure. If you'll please leave now. I'm waiting for a brilliant, and rather late, young man."

Timidly, and with several encouraging prods from Gaston, Sophie said, "No, Professor LaGrange. You are waiting for me."

"You?! Why would I wait for a girl?"

From *Marvels of Math*. © 1998 Kendall Haven. Teacher Ideas Press. (800) 237-6124.

"Because I wrote that paper and signed it M. Le Blanc."

"YOU?!?!" LaGrange's knees trembled a bit, his stomach dropped, and he grasped the door frame for support. "*You* wrote it? But Le Blanc is a . . . I mean he's brilliant. And you're a . . . a girl."

Sophie's cheeks flushed with embarrassment. "I wrote that paper. I borrowed Gaston's notes each evening to study."

LaGrange began to feel faint. He collapsed into an overstuffed chair. "I selected the paper of a girl?!" Then his eyes menacingly bored in on Sophie. His voice turned icy cold and hard. "*Prove* that you wrote it. Let's see if you can answer *my* questions!"

Sophie paled and gulped. "I will do my best, Professor LaGrange."

Forty minutes later, as the faculty and students fidgeted in their seats, Professor Joseph LaGrange emerged from behind the stage curtain, pale and nervous. At his side marched an equally nervous, but very proud, Sophie Germain. The whole auditorium gasped. Professor Monge hissed, "Joseph, what is this? No woman has ever attended this ceremony, much less been its honored award recipient. You can't!"

Sheepishly LaGrange shrugged. "I have to. Both her paper and her mind are truly extraordinary. She's brilliant! She deserves this award more than any student in years."

The shock waves Sophie Germain sent rumbling through the all male scientific community of Europe did not stop with that one award in 1794. In 1816 she won the Grand Prize of the French Academy of Science, awarded by Napoleon Bonaparte, himself. Her papers on the elasticity of solid objects became the foundation for the design of the Eiffel Tower in Paris. Her work on number theory was used in university classrooms for almost two centuries. In 1823, at the age of 47, she was the first woman ever awarded a Doctorate of Science from the University of Göttingen. But, of course, each of those is another story.

Follow-on Questions and Activities to Explore

1. Do you think it was right for women to be automatically excluded from math and science just because they were women? Was it just? Was it fair? Why do you think it was done? Do prejudices still exist which make it harder for women to get into math and science? How can they be done away with?

   Answer: Compare your answers with other students and discuss it as a class.

2. Conduct an experiment. Have the teacher give the class five math problems for every student to solve in the same amount of time. Then see whether the girls or boys got the most questions right. Remember there might not be the same number of girls and boys in your class. You'll have to calculate the *average* number of correct answers per girl, and the average number right per boy for comparison. Were the number correct just about the same for girls and boys? If not, why do you think there was a difference?

   Answer: Compare your answers with other students and discuss it as a class.

Out of Time

At a Glance

Every once in a great while a prodigy is born, someone with such an enormous natural talent in a given field that, even as a child, they excel above all others, amateur or professional. Music has had prodigies. Dance has had them. Painting has had them. And so has mathematics.

Possibly the greatest such mathematical prodigy was born in 1811 in France. He never lived to reach adulthood. He was never able to share his incredible gift for intuitively understanding complex and advanced mathematics. His talent wasn't recognized until long after his premature death. The story of Evarstie Galois is one of the greatest tragedies in the long history of mathematics.

Terms to Know

Understanding the following mathematical terms will help you understand and appreciate this story.

1. **Group Theory.** Group theory is an advanced mathematical technique begun by Evarstie Galois in which algebraic terms and equations are studied not as individual things, but as a whole group of things. The purpose of such study is to identify common properties, axioms, and traits of the group and to classify the members of the group according to group characteristic.

    Group theory is mentioned in this story. But it is not necessary, or even likely, that anyone reading the story will be familiar with group theory, or will even be able to understand Galois' work.

2. **Permutation.** Permutations are all of the different arrangements, or orders of elements within some given set of objects. For example, the three numbers 1, 2, 3 could be arranged six different ways (1-2-3, 1-3-2, 2-1-3, 2-3-1, 3-1-2, and 3-2-1). Thus there are six permutations of the number set 1, 2, 3.

    The number of possible permutations was one of the classification characteristics of groups that Galois studied.

3. **Operation.** The word "operation" is a general term used to describe any mathematical process performed on a number. Addition, subtraction, and multiplication are all operations. So are transformations and integration.

4. **Derivation.** When one function, axiom, theorem, or principal is deduced from another, the process is called a derivation. For example, one of Euclid's axioms was that two intersecting lines create four right angles when they are perpendicular to each other. Many other principles about the nature of right triangles have been deduced, or derived, in part, from this axiom.

Out of Time

"It's after 10 PM already. In seven short hours I will surely die."

"Maybe you won't."

"Ha!" Twenty-year-old Evarstie Galois (Gal-WAH) paced the cluttered, second-floor rented room where he lived. Small and thin, with sad, puppy-dog eyes, he still wore a boy's face and carried a boy's dreams. "I can't shoot. I am no marksman. I am a mathematician. My challenger is an expert in the army. How can I *not* lose the duel?"

"Maybe you'll get lucky. Fire fast and hope for the best." Evarstie's one good friend, twenty-eight-year-old Auguste Chevalier (Shuh-VAL-yea) sprawled across the small couch trying to bolster Galois' spirits and calm his dread. "Maybe he'll miss."

Galois turned on his friend. "Don't you see? This is not a duel about honor. It is not about the girl. I've been set up. The king's men are behind this. They want to *kill* me."

"Then don't go."

"I have to. I've been formally challenged."

"Hide. Run away."

"They are the king's men. They have passes. They will hunt me down."

The date was May 29, 1831. Galois lived in a residential section on the outskirts of Paris, France. The cobbled streets outside still glistened from an afternoon rain. The voices of evening strollers and the clomping of horse hooves drifted through the window, as did the glow from gas streetlamps.

Galois returned to pacing, his hands kneading the air. "If I die, the ideas will die with me. See, I have these ideas about mathematics. By the time I was fourteen I could *see* algebra the way a great composer sees music, the way a mystic sees visions."

Auguste reminded him, "The question for tonight is not math. It is how to survive tomorrow's duel."

From *Marvels of Math.* © 1998 Kendall Haven. Teacher Ideas Press. (800) 237-6124.

"No! The ideas are all that is important. They demand to be heard." Galois paced faster as he talked, speeding almost to a jog as he circled the small, single room. "Clearer than real life, more tangible than the chair you sit in, I could *see* how the roots, or solutions, to algebraic equations formed groups, and how those groups told me things about the original equations. I had no words to describe these groups and the permutations and operations I could perform on them. But I could *see* them in my head. And, even then, the ideas pounded inside me to get out, as if trapped, as if my head were a prison."

Auguste sprang from the couch to grab and shake his friend. "Evarstie! You're babbling!" Auguste coaxed Galois into a chair. "Your ideas are safely recorded, aren't they? You've told me you wrote papers. Surely you've told other mathematicians of your work."

Galois snapped back, "Oh, I have tried to make others listen. I really have."

His face was etched with strain and frustration. "I have reasoned, pleaded, begged, shouted, and cursed. I have written papers that a child should understand. But there are only fools at the French Academy of Sciences and at the University. Fools who are afraid of my genius, my truth!"

"But you *have* written down your ideas," Auguste repeated.

Galois continued, almost without hearing, as he resumed his pacing, as if it were impossible for him to sit still, "And they have always tried to stop me, to ruin me—all of them. But it is not *me*. It is the ideas that demand to be heard.

"Over these last few years the ideas have hounded me, harping at me from inside my head like angry voices, ridiculing my lack of attention, mocking my inability to make others listen, demanding that I let them out. They won't let me sleep. They give me no peace. All because no one will listen."

Galois collapsed, sobbing, onto the couch. "After tomorrow morning I am so afraid no one will ever listen."

Unsure of how to comfort his friend, of how to relieve the fear and torment, Auguste asked, "What ideas are you talking about?"

The tears stopped. Galois looked up, hope and relief spreading across his face. "That's why I asked you to come tonight. I have to tell the ideas to someone. I'm going to tell them to *you*."

From *Marvels of Math.* © 1998 Kendall Haven. Teacher Ideas Press. (800) 237-6124.

"*Me*? But, Evarstie, I don't understand math."

Galois dismissed his friend's protest with a casual wave of his hand. "The ideas are obvious and self-evident. Even a child should be able to follow. Just listen."

"I'll try . . ."

"Everyone is trying to find out how to tell if different forms and orders of algebraic equations are solvable. But they are going at it the wrong way, like mindless fools. I can prove things that will shut down all of their research. The answer lies in examining *groups*. The roots of equations form groups. They must study the groups, not the original equations."

"What groups?" stammered Auguste. "What do you mean by 'root?' I don't understand."

Galois angrily slammed his fist on the long table he used for a desk. "Open your mind, man! Listen! It's so simple! Permutations, or operations, I perform on the groups can tell whether or not the group can be defined, whether the equations can be solved.

"Why can't anyone see this? It's so obvious. A *child* could see."

Auguste wearily rubbed his eyes. "Explain it again, Evarstie. I'll try harder to understand."

Galois's clock began to chime. "It's midnight already. In five hours I must fight a duel I do not want over a girl I hardly know. But it is not about the girl. She is only an excuse. They want to kill me and silence the ideas. They are afraid of my ideas!"

Again he began to sob. "Tonight *I* am afraid."

Auguste gently pushed Galois back into his desk chair. "Rather than telling me the ideas, write them down. Then I'll deliver them to anyone you want."

"Yes, my friend. You are right. I must write. The ideas must get out of my head. I must write them all tonight." Galois snatched a quill pen and stack of blank paper. "But there is no time to write the proofs, the derivations. You must tell them I *had* the proofs. These are not wild ideas. I have the proofs! I should have years to write these theorems, not hours. But no one has ever listened and let me explain."

"No one? Not ever?"

"Believe me, I have tried to make the French Academy, the University, my teachers—all of them—listen. Believe me. I have tried. But they are all against me. They don't want to hear."

"Come, come, Evarstie," said Auguste. "This is only an unfortunate duel. Don't turn it into a grand conspiracy."

Galois' eyes blazed. He slammed down his pen. "*You* don't believe me? Then *you* explain it. At seventeen I failed the entrance exam to the great French University, Ecole Polytechnique. I answered every question correctly and failed. Just because I wouldn't show my work. The problems were trivial. I did them in my head. There was no need to show work. But no one would listen!

"That same year I submitted my first paper to the French Academy of Sciences. The great Chauchy himself promised to read and review my paper. I was so happy! But first he forgot, and then he conveniently lost my work. He never even told me! Explain that."

Auguste stammered, "Well, he's very busy. He *could* have forgotten."

"Then explain this. At eighteen I failed the Ecole Polytechnique entrance exam again. This time I was not even allowed to answer questions. I was teased, taunted, ridiculed by the judges, until I left, sobbing."

"I heard you threw a bucket at one of the judges."

"An eraser. And he deserved it. At nineteen I submitted a magnificent paper carefully explaining my entire theory of groups for the French Academy of Sciences Mathematics Grand Prize Contest. The senior secretary of the Academy himself received my paper. The courier confirmed this. He opened it right away and began to read. But he keeled over dead with a heart attack before completing the first page. Witnesses watched it happen.

"By the time his body was carried away, my paper had vanished. Gone! Never to be read. A year's work! Explain that!"

"Well, of course, I can't. But surely . . ."

Galois cut him off as he continued his tirade. "Earlier this year I submitted yet another paper to the Academy for review. Poisson, the reviewer, refused to read it. Oh, he said he did. But he claimed he couldn't understand. So I know he never touched it in the first place.

"No, they definitely want to stop my ideas. But these ideas will not be silenced!"

Auguste offered, "Maybe you'll only be *wounded* in the duel. I'll get you to a hospital to recover, and then you can write everything down, just the way you want it."

Galois paused and patted his friend's shoulder. "The ideas shriek to be released. I dare not take the chance of survival. They must be heard tonight!"

"But I can't understand a single word of your math! Can't you explain it in arithmetic terms?"

Galois jumped as the clock again chimed. "3 AM. How could it be already? How could this night pass so much quicker than any other?"

Fists pressed to his temples as if to ease the pain of pounding ideas, Galois moaned, "The ideas are clawing at my mind, screeching to be heard. I must write. I must write them all. But there is no time. No time for explanations. No time for proofs. No time for details.

"I must simply present the theorems. Others will have to reconstruct the proofs that are so clear to me. But this is the same others who would not listen when I tried to tell them. How can I trust them now?"

Auguste patiently guided his friend back to his desk chair. "Write them down, Evarstie. Write them down now."

Soon Evarstie looked up from his frantic scrawling. "And now there is no time!"

He crossed his small room and gazed out the window. "The black of night already creeps toward the gray of dawn. Darkness and night have hid the city. Now the gray of death covers it like a shroud. These dull, misty grays of morning look more lovely when I know I'll probably never see them again."

This time they both jumped when the clock chimed.

"It is time. But I am not finished. There are more ideas that must be written. I need more time! But there is no time!

"There must be more time. I must write the ideas . . .but there is no time . . ."

"It is time." The voice, stern and deep, came from outside Galois' door. It was followed by heavy pounding. "Evarstie Galois! Come out for the duel. It is time!"

In the cold, gray mists of the morning of May 30, 1831, twenty-year-old Evarstie Galois lay dying in a small field near the edge of Paris as the first harsh rays of dawn splashed across the City of Lights. His friend, Auguste Chevalier, held his head and his hand and watched the life flow out of him.

Galois lost the duel, his life, and his desperate race with time. For Evarstie Galois, there was no more time.

In the cold, gray mists of the morning of May 30, 1831, twenty-year-old

But the story is not over. In 1870 Camille Jordon finally published Galois' frantic writings of that last night of his life. In the forty years since his death, mathematics had advanced enough for the genius of Galois' ideas to be recognized. The brilliance and power of his theorems swept across Europe.

Now the boy who had been ignored was called the most brilliant mind in the history of mathematics. His work, his hastily written notes from that one night, were hailed as the greatest achievement of all nineteenth-century mathematics.

Single-handedly Galois' work redefined, reshaped, and redirected the path of development for all algebra. His group theory, called the most profound new branch of mathematics in a dozen centuries, has made possible many of the great twentieth-century strides in physics and chemistry.

We can only wonder what Galois could have shown us if he had a lifetime instead of a single night. But that, of course, would be another story.

From *Marvels of Math*. © 1998 Kendall Haven. Teacher Ideas Press. (800) 237-6124.

Follow-on Questions and Activities to Explore

1. What would *you* write down if you had one night to pass on your most important wisdom? What math ideas, theorems, and concepts would you pass on if you had one night to write down the most important concepts you know?

    Answer: Compare your answers with those of other students and discuss your lists as a class.

2. Carefully reread this story. Do you think Evarstie Galois was partly at fault for not being listened to? Do you think he did anything to alienate the mathematics community and undermine his own ideas? What?

    Answer: Compare your answer with those of other students and discuss your ideas as a class.

One Step Forward, One Step Back

*The Theory of Sequences and
Improved Algebraic Solutions
by Sonya Kovalevsky in the 1870s*

At a Glance

During the century after Sophie Germain cracked open the door to mathematics for women, little progress had been made. In the 1860s there were still no mathematics jobs or professorships open to women. There were no research assistantships or teaching assistantships available to women. There were no scholarships or government grants available for women mathematicians. No journal would publish a mathematics paper written by a woman. No award committee would consider an entry from a woman. Only a few universities would admit women as students, and none of those would allow a woman to graduate or grant them a mathematics degree.

Science and math were still considered to be unladylike, and a girl who wanted to learn math was more likely to be punished than encouraged.

This iron fist of prejudice was no where stronger than in Czarist Russia. Still it was in that time, in that country, and from that background that Sonya Kovalevsky fought her way to the top of European mathematics circles, and into the first university mathematics professorship ever granted to a woman.

Terms to Know

Understanding the following mathematical terms will help you understand and appreciate this story.

1. **Calculus.** Calculus is a specific kind of mathematics, as are arithmetic, algebra, geometry, and trigonometry. That is, calculus uses concepts and approaches to solving problems that are unique to calculus. Calculus is generally used for difficult problems that either cannot be solved algebraically, or are very difficult to solve algebraically.

   The key to calculus is that it breaks a problem up into an infinite number of infinitesimally small segments. Isaac Newton first devised a way to easily handle such a vast number of segments by creating a new mathematical technique, called integration. Differentiation, the opposite of integration, and integration are the two basic processes of calculus.

2. **Solution.** When solving arithmetic problems, the word "solution" means "answer." With more advanced problems (some geometry problems, advanced algebra problems, and especially advanced forms of calculus) the term "solution" refers more to the chosen approach or method of solving a problem than to the specific numeric answer. Sonya Kovalevsky made her mark by creating new methods to solve complex problems called partial differential equations.

3. **Equation.** An equation is the general form used to solve algebraic problems. In an equation two mathematical quantities, or terms, are set equal to each other. The equals sign (=) is used to connect the two terms.

   $x = 3a + 2b$ is an equation. It means that the quantity x (whatever that is) is exactly equal to three times whatever a represents plus two times whatever b represents. It is essential to know what is equal to what in solving an algebraic equation.

4. **Partial Differential Equations.** Calculus encompasses two major operations: integration and differentiation. In order to complete either operation on an equation, certain information beyond the equation must be known. Often for differentiation problems, some of this information is missing and the equation can only be partially differentiated. These partial differential equations become some of the most difficult of all equations to solve.

5. **Sequence Theory.** If one number follows another in a logical, defined way, the numbers create a sequence. 1, 2, 3, 4 . . . is a sequence. Each number is one greater than the preceding number. 1, 2, 4, 8, 16 . . . is a sequence. Each number is twice the preceding number. 2, 5, 6.5, 7.25, 7.625 . . . is a sequence. Each number in the sequence (n) equals 1/2 the previous number (n-1) plus 4. X_n is the value of the nth term in the sequence. In equation form, $X_n = 0.5 (X_{n-1}) + 4$. In general if X_n is defined as some function of X_{n-1}, a sequence is created. Sonya Kovalevsky developed new theories on the general form, structure, and use of complex sequences, and devised new methods of manipulating sequences.

One Step Forward, One Step Back

Long, gray-green lines of waves grudgingly split for the straight vertical bow of the new-fangled steamship. Black smoke belched from twin stacks only to be whisked away by stiff winds. The polished wood deck rumbled with the vibrations of the engines and glistened with spray and foam. The ship rhythmically rose and fell as it sliced through each steep wave gliding across the Baltic Sea.

Most passengers lounged inside with the warmth of steam heaters. But one woman braved the biting cold to stand at the rail near the bow. On this dark afternoon of November 5, 1883, the woman, thirty-three-year-old Sonya Kovalevsky (Ko-va-LEV-ski), warily gazed at the slowly growing jagged black line on the horizon, the shoreline of Sweden.

A bank of ugly, black clouds arched up from the southwest, from Denmark. Their rain would strike before the ship reached port in Stockholm.

A shiver raced down Sonya's back, but not from the cold or impending storm. She shivered because of the two newspapers she held, one in each hand.

On any other day Sonya would be described as beautiful. She had creamy skin, dark, sparkling eyes, an infectious smile, and short, stylish brown hair. But here on the deck of this ship, the wind and cold had turned her face blotchy-red, tousled her hair, and some great inner debate, some terrible uncertainty deeply wrinkled her forehead. "Should I get off the ship in Stockholm and begin this new job, or stay on board and crawl back to Russia where it's safe?"

As if a twentieth reading might help her decide, she studied the two papers, their pages snapping in the wind. Both were Stockholm papers. Both were dated November 3, two days ago. In her right hand, the *Stockholm Gazette* editorial praised the appointment of Sonya Kovalevsky as mathematics professor at the new University of Sweden saying, "Today we do not herald the arrival of some vulgar, insignificant prince of noble blood. No, the world's princess of science, Madam Kovalevsky, will honor our city with her arrival, and grace our minds with her mathematics teaching. She will be the first woman lecturer in the history of Sweden."

From *Marvels of Math.* © 1998 Kendall Haven. Teacher Ideas Press. (800) 237-6124.

In her left hand, rival *Stockholm Telegraph* editor, August Strindberg, wrote, "As decidedly as two plus two makes four, what a monstrosity is a woman who attempts to be a professor of mathematics, and how unnecessary, pathetic, injurious, and out of place she is! Drive her back to Russia quickly before we are all shamed and ridiculed by her presence."

Left hand? Right hand? Which paper held the true feelings of this foreign city to Sonya. She sighed and clutched her coat tighter around her throat.

Sonya's five-year-old daughter, Fufa, skipped out onto deck, her blond curls bouncing with each hop. "Fufa! Don't go near the rail. Come to mama!"

Sonya had worried that Fufa wouldn't want to go on this voyage to a new country and home. But Fufa's birthday was October 29. She decided the voyage was really a birthday cruise in her honor, and that after they circled the seas for a while, they'd sail back home. No matter what Sonya said, Fufa refused to believe otherwise.

Shivering next to her mother, little Fufa rocked in cadence with the rise and fall of the ship—one step forward, one step back.

Sonya slowly shook her head. She sadly chuckled. That's how it had always been for Sonya—one step forward, one step back. Every advance of her mathematics career had been met by some cruel force pushing her back. Every triumph had been immediately followed by defeat, every glory by rejection.

Certainly this appointment, a *real* university mathematics professorship, was a huge step forward. What would be waiting here to slap her back?

Again she shivered and glanced at the two opposing editorials. One step forward, one step back. Would she get off the boat and face whatever Stockholm offered, or sail back to Russia and call it Fufa's cruise? Was she up for another struggle? For every step forward it had always been this way.

When Sonya had been nine she became fascinated by mathematics, by the form, order, and logic of equations. Her uncle had offered to tutor her. One step forward.

Her mother wept at a daughter wanting to waste her life. Her father, a Russian general, had punished her for being unladylike, and hired a governess who refused to teach anything more rigorous than needlepoint. One step back.

But Sonya persisted. She had a gift for math. It was as natural for her as words for a gifted writer, as running for a gifted athlete. On her fifteenth birthday, her father relented and gave his permission for Sonya to study this worthless whim of hers. One step forward.

But no Russian academic school would admit a woman. One step back. Three years of private tutors left Sonya hungrier for serious math studies than she was for food, love, marriage, or family.

It was time for another step forward.

Eighteen-year-old Sonya and her twenty-three-year-old sister, Aniuta, huddled in Aniuta's room at the family's spacious country villa outside St. Petersburg. Already considered "old," the pressure was heavy on Aniuta to marry, whether or not she had any desire to do so.

Lounging on her wide bed, Aniuta asked, "Isn't there anything *else* you want to do besides play with the chicken scratches you call equations?"

"No," answered Sonya. "I know this is what I am supposed to do with my life."

"But you're a woman. You can't study math."

"Maybe not in Russia. But I have heard that some German universities allow women to enroll."

Aniuta laughed. "You dreamer! Women aren't allowed to travel alone. Especially *unmarried* women can't go abroad unless accompanied by a parent or guardian. Even if they *were*, our father would never permit it." She sighed, "I want to write about all the places in the world. You want to study mathematics. We are both very good at what we want, but by being born female we are forbidden to do either."

Sonya added, "If we were *sons*, father would shove us out the door to travel and see the world." Then her face brightened into a mischievous grin. "If one of us were married, it *would* be acceptable for us to travel together."

"But then we'd have a husband . . ."

"No," interrupted Sonya. "Find someone willing to be married in name only, just to give us our freedom."

"Who would do that?"

From *Marvels of Math.* © 1998 Kendall Haven. Teacher Ideas Press. (800) 237-6124.

"Through the writing you've published, you know professors and students at St. Petersburg University. Find someone."

Two months later Aniuta found twenty-four-year-old graduate student Vladimir Kovalevsky. One step forward.

The General agreed to consider a proposal for Vladimir to marry Aniuta. But Vladimir only wanted to marry Sonya—provided her father agreed. Their father flatly refused. Aniuta had to be married first, because she was older.

One step back.

Desperate to begin her math studies, Sonya sneaked out of the house, leaving a note saying she had eloped with Vladimir and was already married. Sonya took a carriage to St. Petersburg to stay with friends.

The General was furious and raced after her. But, thinking Sonya had already married, he reluctantly gave his blessing to the marriage. Vladimir, not knowing of Sonya's ruse, heard of her father's consent, and happily married Sonya two weeks later.

"How could you dare to trick father and Vladimir that way?!" exclaimed Aniuta.

"I had to," giggled Sonya.

"I wouldn't dare."

Sonya smiled. "Neither would I. But I did it anyway."

Four months after the marriage, in the blossoming spring of 1869, Sonya, Vladimir, and Aniuta boarded a train to Germany to begin independent lives of study and adventure.

Sonya passed the University of Heidelberg entrance exams without missing a single problem. They readily admitted her as a student in the sciences and mathematics program. One step forward.

One semester later, Sonya was informed that, while she could *study* there, the University would never waste a valuable degree by granting one to a woman. She could study, but would never graduate. One step back.

Infuriated, still hungry for more advanced mathematical challenges, Sonya moved to Berlin where Professor Weierstrass, the greatest of all German mathematicians, taught.

Twice Weierstrass refused to see Sonya because he had no time to waste on a woman. On her third try he gruffly sent her away with a long set of difficult, advanced problems to solve.

"Do *all* your new students have to pass this test?" she asked.

"No. Male students can be admitted with good recommendations from another university."

Sonya bristled. "I have *excellent* recommendations."

"A man can *use* mathematics. The study has *value* for him," answered Weierstrass. "But what can a woman possibly do with math?"

Rich brown eyes blazing, Sonya answered, "I will solve your problems!" and stormed out of the office.

Four days later Sonya returned. To his amazement, Professor Weierstrass found not only that she had correctly solved every problem (a feat many of his most advanced male students could not do), but that many of her solutions (the way she unraveled and solved the problems) were original, exceptionally clear, and, in several cases, superior to his own solutions.

This woman was clearly the most talented student he had ever met. Weierstrass nominated her for admission to study in his program. One step forward.

But the University refused to admit a woman, saying it would embarrass the University and make them easy targets for ridicule.

One step back.

Heartsick at not being able to work with this brilliant mathematical mind, Professor Weierstrass secretly agreed to let Sonya attend his lectures and to tutor her privately as if she were an enrolled student.

By April of 1874, Sonya had accumulated four years of hard study, had become the most advanced math student at the University, and had written eight major papers on mathematics—all under the name "S. Kovalevsky" so that good math journals would publish them. Four of her papers were heralded around Europe as major advances in sequence theory and in differential solutions to advanced algebraic equations. Most assumed such important papers had to have been written by some famed full professor of mathematics.

Two of S. Kovalevsky's papers were used as the basis for teaching advanced mathematics courses at universities across Europe, and were required reading for senior students.

These universities taught Sonya's new theories, but would never have allowed her to enroll and study. The University of Berlin, where Professor Weierstrass taught and Sonya secretly studied, was one of these. They refused to admit her, even though they were the only university that knew she was the brilliant author "S. Kovalevsky."

The University of Berlin mathematics department finally decided they would either have to stop teaching Sonya's theories, or grant her a degree. Sooner or later word would leak out as to who S. Kovalevsky was, and it would look bad for them to be using theories developed by someone who had never graduated from college.

During a prolonged debate, the faculty agreed her theories were too important to omit from their curriculum. Grudgingly, they granted Sonya a Doctorate of Mathematics degree. That spring she became the first woman to receive this highest of all academic degrees from a German university, and the first student to earn a degree without ever enrolling as a student.

Dinners were held in her honor. She packed lecture halls as a guest speaker. One step forward.

Then school ended for the summer. Even with her great fistful of recommendations, even with all her honors, no university—from Portugal to Russia—would hire a woman professor.

One step back.

Sonya was forced to abandon the career she craved and crawl back to Russia to live as ordinary wife and mother. The wall of prejudice blocked her path once again.

Then in 1883, the new University of Stockholm offered Sonya a position as full professor—the first to be offered to a woman in all Europe. At first she wept for joy. A huge step forward.

From *Marvels of Math.* © 1998 Kendall Haven. Teacher Ideas Press. (800) 237-6124.

Then the fears crept into the corners of her thoughts. Nagging doubts raged across her mind. Would another step backward nullify this opportunity? Could she stand another crushing setback?

So Sonya Kovalevsky stood on the deck watching Sweden grow from a dark line on the horizon into mountains, green slopes and fields, crashing waves, and a bustling city. Did she dare to get off the ship?

Even as the horns blew their welcoming blasts and gang-planks were run to the docks, Sonya stood on the deck, unsure of what she should do.

Sonya Kovalevsky taught in Stockholm for eight years. In appreciation and adoration of their mathematics genius, "Sonya" became the most popular girl's name for a whole generation of Swedes.

More importantly, the whole world benefited from Sonya's lifelong struggle. Her papers on sequences and on solving difficult algebraic equations (called partial differential equations) greatly advanced our modern understanding of mathematical operations. Her work also advanced our ability to solve the complex problems that twentieth-century engineers have to solve every time they design a communications system, calculate the design for buildings to withstand earthquake forces, or solve a vast host of other real-world problems. Whether Professor Sonya Kovalevsky was a tough, demanding teacher is another story.

From *Marvels of Math.* © 1998 Kendall Haven. Teacher Ideas Press. (800) 237-6124.

Follow-on Questions and Activities to Explore

1.   Sonya Kovalevsky was the first woman professor of mathematics in the world. Was she the first full-time woman mathematician?

   Answer: No. At least four famous women mathematicians preceded her, Hypatia of ancient Alexandria, Marie Agnesi of early eighteenth-century France, Caroline Hershel of eighteenth-century Germany, and Sophie Germain from late eighteenth-century France. Additionally, many part-time mathematicians, including at least thirty of Pythagoras' famed Brotherhood, were women.

2.   Who (and when) was the first U.S. woman mathematics professor? Who was the first U.S. female professor of any subject? What percentage of current U.S. mathematics professors are women?

   Answer: Use your school and public library, the Internet, and the resources of the National Women's History Project (Windsor, CA) to find your answers. Compare your answers with other students and discuss as a class the progress women have made into the math and science fields.

Stories
About
Calculating
Machines

No Bones About It!

The Invention of "Napier's Bones"
by John Napier in 1605

At a Glance

The Scotsman John Napier is best known for inventing logarithms, a system for reducing complex multiplication problems to easy addition. John Kepler once said that Napier "doubled the life of every astronomer" with his invention of natural logarithms.

Napier is also remembered for inventing the idea of separating a whole number from its fractional part with a dot, or period. All of John Napier's inventions followed the same theme—make practical math quicker and easier to do. His first invention was one of his most interesting and time saving devices. It was also the first improvement on an abacus in two thousand years. The invention was commonly called "Napier's Bones." This is the story of the Bones' invention.

Terms to Know

Understanding the following mathematical terms will help you understand and appreciate this story.

1. **Exponent.** The use of power notation (a^2, a^3, etc.) is shorthand for repetitive multiplication. a^2 tells you to multiply two of whatever a represents together (a times a). The "2" is called an exponent. a^3 tells you to multiply three of whatever a represents together (a x a x a). a^4 tells you to multiply four a's together (a x a x a x a). You do not need to always raise some quantity to a whole number power. You could write exponents with decimal parts. $a^{3.2}$ means (a x a x a x a/5). Archimedes was the first to use exponential notation to indicate raising a number to some power.
   $x^2 = 16$ is a simple algebraic problem using exponents.

2.   Logarithm. Logarithms are a special use of exponents. Archimedes found that if he could express two numbers as exponents of the same base number (100 as 10^2 and 10,000 as 10^4, for example), he could multiply the numbers together by adding their exponents. $2 + 4 = 6$. So the answer was 10^6 or 1,000,000. John Napier got the idea to express *every* number as an exponent for some common base, say 10. Since $10 = 10^1$, the logarithm (or "log") of 10 is 1. $100 = 10^2$, so its log is 2. $25 = 10^{1.398}$, so its log is 1.398. Any two numbers may be multiplied by adding their logarithmic (or "log") values.

This story about John Napier does not directly involve his invention of logarithms. But they are mentioned, as are some of the concepts which led him to that invention.

No Bones About It!

In 1605 Edinburgh was a city by Scottish standards. It was a muddy slum by English standards. A heavy, stone castle stood atop a steep but rolling hill leading out of Edinburgh to the north, Merchiston Castle. Along the east wall of this castle a tower rose from the main hall to pierce the sky. Its windows faced into the rising sun. The Napier (NAY-pee-er) family crest fluttered on a banner from the tower.

Fifty-five-year-old John Napier, Lord of Merchiston, owned all the houses and buildings, all the vast tracts of rolling fields, all the cattle and the cows, the entire vast estate of Merchiston. But his great holdings, and the power they brought, gave John little pleasure. His passions were saved for writing stories, for treasure hunts, and especially for mathematics.

John Napier did not love math for math's sake. He saw little value in analyzing spheres, ellipses, and algebraic functions. No, John Napier loved math because it gave ordinary people the power to figure out necessary quantities and sums. It let them solve everyday problems. Napier loved math because it was practical and useful.

John Napier was not a broad-shouldered, powerful highlander. His kilt hung on thin hips and revealed knobby knees and skinny legs. His shoulders drooped. But his eyes sparkled with excitement behind his gray beard, as if a new idea flashed into his mind every few seconds.

On a warm afternoon in August 1605, with only the faintest few puffs of white cotton drifting across a deep blue sky, John Napier paced across one of the castle rooms that he had converted into an accounting office. Before him, two bookkeepers furiously scribbled in their ledgers. The only sounds were the rapid scraping of quill pens, the faint sounds of field work drifting through the wide windows, the buzzing of hungry summer flies, and the sounds of John's children (twelve-year-old Archibald and six-year-old Janet) reciting their lessons in the next room.

For the fifth time in an hour, John slowed his pacing and peered over one bookkeeper's shoulder. "Have you got the final figures yet, William?"

The scribe neither glanced up nor paused in his frantic multiplication. "Not yet, sire."

From *Marvels of Math*. © 1998 Kendall Haven. Teacher Ideas Press. (800) 237-6124.

"And you, James?"

"Not in the past five minutes. No, sir."

"What's taking so long?" Napier demanded.

"This is not simple work, sir," said James. "There's lots of multiplication and division—and with very large numbers."

"And we have to make sure there are no errors," added young William. "One error would ruin everything."

Old James, who started as a castle bookkeeper for John Napier's father when John was but a wee baby, added, "Your father let us lump the grain harvest from all the fields together when we made our calculations. It went much faster."

"You must calculate exactly how many tons of oats per acre were harvested for each field *separately*," insisted Lord Napier. "I'm testing different growing methods in each field. By next year I'll have discovered how to produce the biggest possible crop of oats. There will be no more guessing or supposing."

Twenty-two-year-old William said, "You already produce more oats than any other lands in the county." Young William glanced nervously at his employer before continuing, "In town they say you cast spells from your tower to make your oats grow faster."

John threw back his head and laughed. "Do they now? My only 'spell' is called close observation and thoughtful experimentation." Again he began to pace. "But I need to see figures for our oat production in each field before I can decide which system works best."

"As soon as we finish the calculations, my lord," said James.

Exasperated, John Napier pounded one fist into his other palm. "It is intolerable for an idea, for progress, to be held up by simple multiplication!"

"It's not that simple," muttered William.

Napier turned toward the circular stone stairs leading toward his tower study. "Maybe I should invent an easier way to multiply."

As the echo of his footsteps faded, William said, "Maybe he'll cast a spell up there and make the numbers multiply themselves."

From *Marvels of Math.* © 1998 Kendall Haven. Teacher Ideas Press. (800) 237-6124.

John Napier stood at his tower window and gazed across the miles of newly-mowed fields. He said the words to the clouds, as if passing puffs of water vapor would care, as if they might answer. "Multiplication is tedious and slow, especially with large numbers. Addition is easy and quick. If I could turn multiplication into addition, and division into subtraction, I would make calculations much easier and faster—but how?"

John slumped into a chair at the long table he used for à desk. Copies of other mathematicians' papers were strewn across its surface, as was a detailed floor plan of Fastcastle in Berwickshire, where John and Robert Logan planned to dig for buried treasure. Charts, ledgers, and books were stacked along one wall.

John idly tapped a compass against a stack of writing paper. "How odd. Mankind invented multiplication because repetitive addition was too slow. Now multiplication is too slow, and I'm trying to find a way to turn it back into addition because that would be faster."

A memory snapped to the front of his mind. He rummaged through shelves of monograms, reports, and papers. "Even Archimedes hinted at being able to turn some kinds of multiplication into addition. Now where was it? He wrote 10 as 10^1, 100 as 10^2, 1000 as 10^3, and so on. The 1, 2, and 3 he called exponents, or the number of times ten had to be multiplied by itself to equal a certain number."

He held up an ancient, handwritten report and thumbed through the pages. "Ah, yes. Here it is. To multiply 100 times 10,000, Archimedes wrote the numbers in exponential form (10^2 X 10^4) and then *added* the exponents. $2 + 4 = 6$. So the answer is 10^6, or 1,000,000."

John set down the paper and tapped it with his finger. "This has promise. He was able to turn a multiplication problem into an addition one. But I can't see yet how it will solve the problems of ordinary multiplication."

"Who are you talking to, father?" Napier's son stood at the tower doorway.

"Archibald! Come in. I was just talking to myself." Napier began to laugh. "Oh, don't look so worried. It doesn't mean I've gone mad, or that I've become a wizard."

"I've heard the lads in town say you *are* a wizard, father."

"They're mistaking brain power for magic." Napier paused and then brightened as a new idea and a fresh direction flashed into his mind. "Archibald, I need to better understand multiplication. Can you teach me how to do it?"

Archibald looked even more worried. "You *have* gone daft, father. You already know multiplication better than anyone. You taught *me* how to multiply."

"Yes, yes, I know. But it would help me to watch you work carefully and slowly through the steps."

Archibald shrugged, flopped into a chair, and dipped a quill into the inkwell. "What should I multiply?"

"Anything will do. Try 463 times 78."

Archibald sighed, as if maybe the local boys were right. "First I multiply 463 times 8."

His father stopped him as soon as he began to write. "No, son. Tell me *everything* you do."

Archibald rolled his eyes. "All right, father. First I multiply 3 times 8 which is 24. So, I write the 4 here and carry the 2."

"Where do you carry it to?" asked John.

"I just carry it in my head. But I suppose I could write it above the next column."

"One digit is always written in the first column, and one is carried to the next. Very good. Go on."

Again Archibald sighed with worry. "Now I multiply 8 times the next number, 6. That's 48. But I carried 2 from before. So now I add that to 48 and get 50. So I write the 0 in the second column and carry the 5."

John Napier clapped his son on the back. "Thank you, Archibald. That is *exactly* how you do it. Already you have shown me two important things."

"I have?"

"First, we never multiply big numbers together!"

"Yes, we do, father. William and James are multiplying *huge* numbers downstairs."

"No, they are not," corrected John. "At each moment we only multiply one digit by one other digit. We just do it lots of times. Think of it! All of multiplication is just 1 through 9 times 1 through 9!"

"What about 12 or 13?" asked Archibald.

"That's just 1 in the tens column times something, and 2 in the ones column times something. Don't you see?"

"I think so father. But, so what?"

Lord Napier paused, his left hand waving slowly in the air, as if groping for the right words. "I—I don't know yet. But it will combine somehow with the second thing you showed me. A single digit times a single digit always produces only one digit to write down. Often there is a second digit that is carried to the next column. But those are the only two possibilities.

"It's the same every time. And it's so very simple! It's time consuming because we do the same simple thing over and over so many times in a large multiplication problem."

Napier began to pace. "I should be able to create something to make the process easier. But what?"

"But what?" repeated Archibald.

Lord Napier motioned for his son to leave the tower. "Thank you for your help, Archibald. Now I have to think."

A week later, John Napier rushed into his accounting room with a cloth bag filled with what sounded like rattling bones.

William shuttered. "He's been castin' bones up there! It's spells for sure!"

"No, it's ivory strips," corrected John, pouring the bag onto William's work table. "I used ivory because it will last longer than wood or paper."

"What is it, my lord?" asked James, peering at the pile of ivory strips. Each was eight inches long and two inches wide with numbers written down its length.

Napier said, "Look at it this way, James. Let's say you are multiplying one number times another and there is a six in the first number."

Napier picked up the ivory strip with a large "6" at the top. Below the 6, nine boxes were drawn on the strip, stacked on top of each other. In the top box a "6" was written. In the second box was a "12" with a diagonal line, "/," separating the "1" and the "2." A "1" and an "8" were written in the third box, again separated by a diagonal slash. And so on.

"There are only nine numbers you can multiply times that six, the digits 1 through 9," John continued. "In the nine boxes on these strips I've already done those possible multiplications. Don't you see? All you have to do is add, and any difficult multiplication is done."

Napier smiled with satisfaction.

His two bookkeepers gazed with wonder and confusion. "But, how do they work, my lord? Do I say a magic spell?" whispered William.

John said, "When you multiply one digit times another, you always write only one digit down. Correct?"

Both bookkeepers nodded.

"Sometimes there is a second digit you carry to the next column. You write down one digit, and carry one digit to the next column. See the diagonal line across each box on the strips? That line separates the digit you write down from the digit you carry."

"But how do they work, my lord?" repeated James.

"I'll show you. James, give us a problem. William, I'll race you."

James rubbed his chin. "Very well. 7362 times 249."

William jotted the numbers and began to multiply. "Nine times two is eighteen. Carry the one . . ."

From *Marvels of Math*. © 1998 Kendall Haven. Teacher Ideas Press. (800) 237-6124.

Lord Napier placed four ivory strips side by side, one for the seven, one for the three, one for the six, and one for the two, 7 - 3 - 6 - 2. "There is the first number." He began to write the digits from across several rows of the four strips. "The 9th row, the 4th row times 10 for the ten's column, and the 2nd row times 100 for the hundred's column."

William redipped his pen. "Nine times seven is sixty-three, plus the three I carried . . ."

"The answer is 1,833,138," announced Napier.

William was stunned. "I barely finished the first line of multiplications! It's magic for sure."

"No. It's brain power and simple observation," corrected Napier.

James nodded, "I think I see how those bones work, my lord. May I try them?"

"I made a complete set for each of you," said Napier. "Now, maybe I can get my crop figures out on time."

"On time if not before, sir," smiled James as he slid five strips next to each other for a problem he was working on. "8 - 3 - 4 - 1 - 7" he began.

William seemed almost afraid to touch his set. "I still say there must be a spell on them bones!"

∾ ∾ ∾

That day, in 1605, John Napier laid out the world's first calculator, Napier's Bones. Napier's later use of the natural logarithm led others to combine the concepts of logarithms and sliding ivory strips to create the first slide rule.

A century and a half later, the ideas John Napier built into his simple strips helped Charles Babbage and Ida Lovelace design the world's first mechanical computing engine (computer). But that fascinating development is another story.

From *Marvels of Math*. © 1998 Kendall Haven. Teacher Ideas Press. (800) 237-6124.

Follow-on Questions and Activities to Explore

1. Make a set of Napier's Bones and use them to solve the multiplication problem
   7239 x 47. A sample problem is shown (page 151) for you to use as a guide. In-
   structions are below.

   Answer: Compare your answer with those of other students and discuss the
   technique as a class.

2. Was it faster for you to use Napier's Bones than to do multiplication long hand?
   What would make the Bones even faster? Could you *divide* using Napier's
   Bones?

   Answer: Napier's bones only work for multiplication. He never developed a set
   of aids for division.

INSTRUCTIONS

   Napier's strips, or "Bones" do the multiplication for you. All you have to
do is add.

   To record a product, say 7239 x 47 from the example problem, you need
only write down the results of the individual multiplications (4 x 9, 4 x 3, 4 x 2,
and 4 x 7)—all already written along the "4" row of Napier's Bones. Remember, Napier discovered that, for each multiplication, we write down one digit
and carry one digit to be added to the next column. Re-read the story for his
explanation.

   For this example of 7239 x 47, start with the right-hand column of the
"four" row. Write down the 6. In the second column write down the "2," but
remember to add the "3" carried from the 1st column. Thus you write a "5."
Notice that you are adding the two numbers in a diagonal row going from
upper-right to lower-left. In the third column write 8 plus 1 carried from the 2nd
column, or "9." Write "8" in the fourth column since nothing is carried from the
3rd column. Finally write the carried "2" into the fifth column.

   Thus you write 28956 for the answer of 7239 x 4. But the "4" in the original multiplication problem is in the *tens* position. You must therefore multiply
your answer by ten, or really write 289560 as the answer to 7239 x 40.

   Repeat the process for the seven row and add the results to obtain your
final answer.

Using Napier's Bones to multiply.

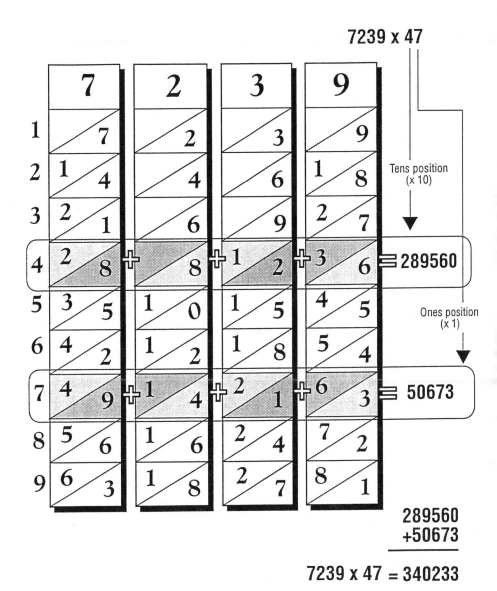

7239 x 47

289560
+50673
───────
7239 x 47 = 340233

Amazing Grace

The Invention of Computer Languages
by Grace Hopper in 1944

At a Glance

Arithmetic computations are hard, and often time-consuming. They are repetitive and exacting. Every individual calculation must be performed *exactly* right. Even a simple multiplication problem like 376 x 284 involves over thirty separate steps and calculations.

As long as humans have performed these complex mathematical calculations, they have sought the assistance of machines to make the job easier.

The first mechanical device developed to help perform math was the abacus. Devices like an abacus were drawn in the sand for individual computations by early Babylonians. Some clever, unknown Egyptian was the first to build a wood and metal abacus that could be carried from place to place and computation to computation. From Egypt the abacus spread throughout Europe and as far east as China. For fifteen hundred years the abacus was the primary calculating device known to humankind.

In the early part of the seventeenth century the Scot, John Napier, created an early version of a slide rule, called "Napier's Bones." Made of ivory or wood, these strips could slide next to each other to perform large parts of multiplication problems. By the end of that century, formal slide rules were in existence and in use throughout Europe.

All of these devices, however, can perform calculations only as fast as human fingers can physically move beads or slides. The first step toward a true computing machine came in the mid-nineteenth century, when Englishman Charles Babbage envisioned a wondrous machine, capable of performing all of the necessary steps of a complex calculation on its own. Babbage could see the machine in his head. He could draw it on paper. But he could not build it because of material limitations and a lack of manufacturing precision in the factories of the day.

While Babbage envisioned the hardware, his assistant, Ida Lovelace, recognized the need to create simple, repetitive groups of commands to make the machine run efficiently. He created the first plans for a computer. She created the first inklings of a computer language.

A century later, mathematicians at Harvard University and at the IBM Corporation combined to build a calculation machine, the Mark I, based on Babbage's design. These technicians were so focused on building the enormous hardware of the computer, they put little thought into the language, or command system, they would use to direct and communicate with the beast.

That's when mathematics professor Grace Hopper entered the picture.

Terms to Know

Understanding the following mathematical terms will help you understand and appreciate this story.

1. **Computer.** A computer is any machine designed to compute or calculate. The first computer, the Mark I, was built in 1943-44 and could make only three calculations per second. (This speed, however, was considered amazingly fast at the time.) Modern computers can make millions of calculations per second.

    The label "computer" is commonly used to mean that the machine can be redirected by some commands or programs to perform whole new routines. A calculator, on the other hand, can only perform the calculations it was built to perform and cannot be reprogrammed to perform any other tasks.

2. **Computer Language.** An operator needs to be able to talk to a computer in order to tell it what it is supposed to do. When you want to tell something to someone else, you need words (a language). You have to know the language to be able to put the ideas in your head into words, and the listener needs to know the same language to understand your words and know what they mean.

    The same is true for talking to a computer. Someone has to create a language that the programmer and the computer can both understand. Then directions and commands can be worded in this special language and the computer will understand what to do. These languages are called computer languages.

    Some computer languages direct the machine to perform very basic operations (turn itself on, retrieve start-up programs from memory, be able to read other commands entered from a keyboard, etc.) Some languages are used to tell the computer how to perform necessary computations (how to alphabetize a list of names, how to calculate a square root, etc.).

    The programmers who create computer languages must work very closely with the people who build computers to make sure that the computers can understand and interpret the various commands, terms, and symbols in the language.

3. **Ordinance.** As used in the military, ordinance refers to all large guns and their shells. Mostly ordinance refers to cannons and their various types of explosive shells and projectiles.

Amazing Grace

"You're late!" The man with a high forehead, close-cropped hair, and small, tight mouth glared at her from behind his desk as she fumbled with her briefcase and a stack of orders and directions.

The hum of distant machinery rumbled through this basement room, as did the buzz of banks of overhead fluorescent lights that glared down, creating dazzling reflections on the polished linoleum floor. The stifling heat of July 2, 1944, had wormed its way even down here into this buried cellar world.

"Is this the right basement for the Navy Bureau of Ordinance Computation Project?" she asked, trying to gather her belongings into her left hand so she could salute with her right. Her trim, brown hair squeezed out from under her navy officer's hat.

"You're in the navy. It's a *deck*, not a basement. And you're late." The pencil clamped in his teeth wiggled up and down as he talked.

Her cheeks blushed bright red. "I'm Lieutenant JG Grace Hopper and I'm looking for Professor Howard Aiken."

"I'm *Commander* Aiken to you. We're *all* in the navy here. Now why are you late?"

This was not how thirty-seven-year-old Grace had envisioned that her first meeting with her first commander on her first navy assignment would go. Flustered, she tried to click her heels and salute. "Sir, I had to report to district headquarters in Boston. It took *four* offices to tell me where the Bureau of Ordinance Computation Project was. It took two just to find out *what* it was. Then it took me three hours to get to Harvard and find Cruft Laboratory and figure out how to get down here into this basement."

"I don't mean *today*."

Grace was taken aback. "I was with my parents this weekend, sir, after graduation on Friday."

Commander Aiken rose and pounded the desk with his finger to emphasize each word. Grace Hopper stood barely five feet, so her commander now towered over her. "You're *two months* late, Lieutenant! I needed you *before* you went to midshipman's school when this project was first being assembled."

From *Marvels of Math*. © 1998 Kendall Haven. Teacher Ideas Press. (800) 237-6124.

A shock trembled through Lt. Hopper. *Two months* late?! This was not going well at all. "I . . . I didn't know . . . My orders said . . ."

But Aiken was already marching toward double doors at one end of this office room. "I hope you're ready to work."

"Yes, sir!"

"Has anyone told you about Mark I?"

"Mark who?"

Aiken stopped at the doors and spun back to face Grace. "Not *who*, it's a *what*. Mark I is a computing engine."

He threw open the double doors and led Grace into a much larger room marked "Restricted. Authorized Access Only." Before her stood Mark I, the world's first computer. Over fifty feet long and eight feet high, Mark I was endless banks of black metal boxes in gray metal frames with columns of floor to ceiling lights. Each panel was enclosed in a glass case which could be opened for access and maintenance. Five hundred miles of wire and 800,000 parts were magically woven together to make calculations at the undreamed speed of three computations per second!

A four horsepower motor whined in back of the main console driving the fifty-foot-long main shaft. Mark I was an electro-mechanical machine. That is, it used bulky mechanical switches to store and process data instead of vacuum tubes, transistors, or microchips.

Two navy ensigns busily monitored the monster as it hummed, clicked, and whirred. An enlisted man prepared punch cards on what looked like an overgrown typewriter.

With 4,000 mechanical relays clicking open and closed, it sounded to Grace like an auditorium full of people quietly knitting.

Aiken nodded toward the ensigns. "As soon as they're through with this problem, you're on."

Grace stared at this wondrous sight straight out of science fiction stories. Over one hundred years ago Englishman Charles Babbage dreamed of such a machine. He even drew simple designs. But he couldn't build one because his world lacked the materials and manufacturing precision and know-how to match his designs.

From *Marvels of Math.* © 1998 Kendall Haven. Teacher Ideas Press. (800) 237-6124.

But here it stood a century later, a mathematician's dream on the basement floor—er, deck—before her. "What can it do?" she asked, like a breathless, eager car buyer.

"That's what you're here to find out. Your first job will be to calculate the coefficients for the interpolation of the arc tangent."

"When do you need them?" asked Grace. As a mathematics professor, she knew what these coefficients were and what they were for.

Aiken pushed back through the double doors. Over his shoulder he said, "You're already late. They were due last Wednesday."

Rooted where she stood next to the door, Grace Hopper's awe-filled eyes stared at the gleaming Mark I, and, at this first sight, she fell in love with this whirling dervish, this knit-clicking marvel. Reverently she tiptoed forward as if in a cathedral. She reached out to touch it cautiously with only one finger at first, as if it were alive, as it rumbled, hummed, flashed, and clicked.

Grace knew of Babbage's work and designs. His manuscripts read like science fiction, like science dream. Spitting out answers before her stood the reality of the world's first computer, all based on Babbage's ideas.

The hardware had been built over the past year as a joint project of Professor Aiken of Harvard, the IBM Corporation, and the Navy. But in their rush to create the computing machine, itself, no one had thought much about how they would communicate with this mechanical marvel, how they would command and control it. Grace Hopper had been brought in both to work *on* the Mark I, and to explore better ways to work *with* the beast.

The two ensigns stopped their work, jokingly elbowed each other and nodded toward Grace. "Here to meet our temperamental baby?" asked tall, slender Richard Bloch.

Shorter, chunkier Robert Campbell said, "It's quite a gadget." And then added, "*If* you like to spend most of your time coaxing it to work."

"I'm going to be working on the Mark I," said Grace, extending her hand to formally meet her new co-workers.

"*Another* woman," groaned Bloch.

"There are other women here?" asked Grace.

"A white-haired school teacher who'll probably rap our knuckles with a ruler every time this contraption breaks down," nodded Campbell. "But she's two months late already."

"That's me," laughed Grace. Then she tried to look stern. "And that's Lieutenant Hopper to you, ensign!"

But even before the ensigns could snap back a "Yes, ma'am!" Grace broke out laughing again. "Actually, it's just Grace."

They offered to give Grace a complete tour of the beast. "We know it better than anyone," bragged Bloch.

Campbell grimaced and nodded. "That's because we spend more time fixing it than running it. So will you. It's not the most dependable machine."

At first Grace's heart thumped and seemed to catch up in her throat. *Me? Take care of all this?*

Then she forced a deep breath and whispered to herself, "I can do this."

Two childhood memories flashed through her mind. For years her favorite toy had been a Structiron construction kit of nuts, bolts, and metal girders. As a seven-year-old she had once taken apart all seven bedroom alarm clocks in the family's rambling summer house at the lake. She hadn't been able to put any of them back together, and she never quite figured out how they worked, but she was a pro at taking them apart!

"I can do this!" Still running her hands over the banks of lights and switches, she added, "This machine is beautiful—more than beautiful, it's glamorous."

"Wow. I think we have a convert." And both ensigns chuckled.

Grace asked, "How do you tell it what to do?"

"Write code."

"What's code?"

Bloch said, "We have to write every detail of each step of every computation in number codes. Those codes get transferred onto punched cards that Mark I can read."

Grace asked, "Who designed the system of codes?"

"That's the problem," admitted Campbell. "A few code commands were hardwired into the machine, like the command to add two numbers. (That's 07.) We're trying to create and add more as we go. But it's sort of hodge-podge."

An excited gleam flashed across Grace's eyes. Again she whispered to herself, "I can do this." To the ensigns she said. "Leave it to a woman. Women have always written the codes for computing machines."

Bloch laughed, "Since this is the first computation machine in the world, and you're the first woman here. How can that be?"

"Read your history, ensign," smiled Grace. "If Charles Babbage designed the first computing engine, his assistant, Ida Lovelace, recognized the need for groups of basic, repetitive commands. She wrote the first codes, even though Babbage couldn't build his machine to use them."

From that first day, Grace Hopper was enthralled by the challenge of designing better, more efficient command codes for Mark I and for its successor Mark II. Still, much of her time was spent fixing relays that jammed, stuck, or shorted. They would have to turn out all the room lights and grope along the length of the back of Mark I searching for the telltale tiny sparks that gave away a failed relay. More often than not, the problems were caused by moths and other flying bugs that flew into the machine and were pounded to death by the mechanical relays until they shorted out, or gummed up, the switch. Soon everyone called the process of cleaning them out "debugging" the computer.

◌◌◌◌◌◌

Grace Hopper went on to design codes (they changed the word to "program" because they thought it sounded more impressive) for ENIAC, BINAC, and UNIVAC computers, the UNIVAC being the first mass-produced, commercially available computer in the world. Besides writing programs, Grace was a true pioneer in designing and developing whole languages for computers including COBAL, the most successful general purpose business and accounting program for over thirty years.

It is interesting that while the builders of early computer hardware were men, the first two great programmers, Ida Lovelace and Grace Hopper, were both women. But that's another story.

Follow-on Questions and Activities to Explore

1. Pretend you have been given a very simple computer with very limited capabilities. You need to program it to make several calculations for you. All you have been given is a sample program—once used to increase the numbers in two memory locations by 12. (Shown below.) You are also handed a list of the nine functions that the computer has been built to understand. They are:

00	Stops the computer
01	Starts the computer and zeroes out the main calculation register (location 001)
02	Tells the computer to move a number from the first location mentioned to the second
03	Add
04	Subtract
05	Multiply
06	Divide
07	Square Root
08	Decide if the number in main register is greater than zero

    Here is the sample program you were given.

First Location	Operation	Second Location
	01	
224	02	001
001	03	(12)
001	02	224
225	02	001
001	03	(12)
001	02	225
	00	

    Here is your problem: There are important numbers in memory locations 261 through 268 that are in the wrong units. The first four are listed in feet, but are supposed to be in inches. The last four are listed in meters but are supposed to be in inches. Write a program to convert all eight amounts to the correct units.

    Answer: Compare your program listing with those of other students and discuss it as a class.

2. What was hard about this language? Was it unnecessarily slow and time-consuming? Do you think you could design a better computer language (a system of communication with the machine) than the one in use for question 1? What would your language look like? What would you want to be able to say to the computer? What do you want your computer to be able to do?

    Answer: Compare your answer with other students and discuss it as a class.

References

The selected references for this book are listed here rather than separately for each story because most include information on more than one of the mathematicians. This list includes all of the major references I used and selected samplings of my smaller, mathematician-specific, but still publicly-available references. This list should satisfy most curiosities about the mathematicians mentioned in this book. Not all of them will be available through any one library. Check with your local librarian for additional references that your library has to offer.

Aaboe, Asger. *Episodes from the Early History of Mathematics.* Washington, DC: Mathematical Association of America, 1964.

Abbott, David. *The Biographical Dictionary of Scientists: Mathematicians.* New York: Peter Bedrick, 1986.

Adler, Albert. "Mathematics and Creativity." *The New Yorker* (Feb. 19, 1972): 68–77.

Aiton, E. J. *Liebniz: A Biography.* Boston: A. Hilger, 1984.

Anderson, K. "The Mathematical Technique in Fermat's Deduction of the Law of Refraction." *Historia Mathematica* 10 (1983): 48–62.

Asimov, Isaac. *Realm of Numbers.* Boston: Houghton Mifflin, 1969.

Ball, W. W. Rouse. *A Short Account of the History of Mathematics.* New York: Dover, 1960.

Beckman, Peter. *A History of Pi.* New York: St. Martin's, 1977.

Bell, E. T. *Men of Mathematics.* (2 vols). New York: Penguin, 1963.

Beshore, George. *Science in Ancient Islamic Culture.* New York: Franklin Watts, 1988.

Billings, Charlene. *Grace Hopper, Navy Admiral and Computer Pioneer.* Hillside, NJ: Enslow, 1989.

Bos, H. J. "On the Representation of Curves in Descartes' Geometrie." *Archive for History of Exact Science* 24 (1981): 295–338.

Boyer, Carl B., and Uta Merzbach. *A History of Mathematics.* New York: John Wiley, 1989.

Burton, David M. *The History of Mathematics.* Boston: Allyn & Bacon, 1985.

Cajori, Florian. *A History of Mathematical Notations.* La Salle, IL: The Open Court, 1978.

———. *A History of Mathematics.* New York: Chelsea House, 1985.

Calinger, R. *Gottfried Leibniz.* Troy, NY: Rensselear Polytechnic Institute, 1976.

Campbell, W. "An Application from the History of Mathematics." *Mathematics Teacher* 70 (1977): 538–40.

Clagett, M. *Archimedes in the Middle Ages.* (5 vols). Philadelphia: American Philosophical Society, 1963–1984.

Clark, Ronald. *Einstein: The Life and Times.* New York: Avon, 1979.

Cohen, I. B. *Introduction to Newton's Principia.* Cambridge, MA: Cambridge University Press, 1971.

Cohen, M. R. *A Source Book in Greek Science.* Cambridge, MA: Harvard University Press, 1958.

Court, N. "Desargues and His Strange Theorem." *Scripta Mathematica* 20 (1964): 5–13, 155–64.

Dantzig, T. *Numbers: The Language of Science.* New York: Doubleday, 1974.

Datta, B., and A. Singh. *History of Hindu Mathematics.* Bombay: Asia Publishing House, 1972.

Dedron, P. *Mathematics and Mathematicians.* New York: Transworld, 1971.

Dunham, William. *Journey Through Genius: The Great Theorems of Mathematics.* New York: John Wiley, 1990.

Edwards, Harold. *Fermat's Last Theorem: A Genetic Introduction to Algebraic Number Theory.* New York: Springer-Verlag, 1977.

Erhardt, E. von. "Archimedes' Sand-Reckoner." *Isis* 33 (1962): 578–602.

Eves, Howard W. *An Introduction to the History of Mathematics*, 6th ed. New York: Saunders College, 1990.

——. *Great Moments in Mathematics (Before 1650).* Washington, DC: Mathematical Association of America, 1980.

——. *Great Moments in Mathematics (After 1650).* Washington, DC: Mathematical Association of America, 1983.

Fauvel, J., and J. Gray, eds. *The History of Mathematics: A Reader.* New York: Macmillan Education/Open University, 1987.

Field, J. V. *The Geometrical Work of Girard Desargues.* New York: Springer-Verlag, 1987.

Fowler, D. "Book II of Euclid's Elements and a Pre-Eudoxan Theory of Ratio." *Archive for History of Exact Science* 26 (1982): 193–209.

Gay, Kathlyn. *Science in Ancient Greece.* New York: Franklin Watts, 1988.

Grinstein, Louise S., and Paul Campbell. *Women of Mathematics: A Biological Sourcebook.* New York: Greenwood, 1987.

Gupta, R. "Sine of Eighteen Degrees in India up to the Eighteenth Century." *Indian Journal of the History of Science* 11 (1) (1976): 1–10.

Hall, A. R. *Philosophies at War: The Quarrel Between Newton and Leibniz.* Cambridge, MA: Cambridge University Press, 1980.

Heath, T. *A History of Greek Mathematics.* (2 vols). New York: Dover, 1981.

Hollingdale, Stuart. *Makers of Mathematics.* New York: Penguin Books, 1989.

Ifrah, Georges. *From One to Zero.* New York: Viking Press, 1985.

Kitcher, P. "Fluxions, Limits, and Infinite Littleness. A Study of Newton's Presentation of the Calculus." *Isis* 64 (1973): 33–49.

Kline, Morris. *Mathematics in Western Culture.* New York: Penguin, 1972.

——. *Mathematics and the Physical World.* New York: Dover, 1989.

Knorr, W. *The Evolution of the Euclidean Elements.* Boston: Reidel, 1975.

——. "Archimedes and the Measurement of the Circle: A New Interpretation." *Archive for History of Exact Science* 15 (1976): 115–40.

——. "Archimedes and the Spirals. The Heuristic Background." *Historia Mathematica* 5 (1978): 43–75.

——. "Archimedes and the Pre-Euclidean Proportion Theory." *Archives Internationales d'Historie des Sciences* 28 (1978): 183–44.

Kramer, Edna. *The Main Stream of Mathematics*. New York: Oxford University Press, 1974.

———. *The Nature and Growth of Modern Mathematics*. Princeton, NJ: Princeton University Press, 1981.

Lenoir, T. "Descartes and the Geometrization of Thought." *Historica Mathematica* 6 (1979): 355–79.

Libbrecht, U. *Chinese Mathematicians Through the Thirteenth Century*. Cambridge, MA: MIT Press, 1973.

Mahoney, M. *The Mathematical Career of Pierre de Fermat*. Princeton, NJ: Princeton University Press, 1973.

Meschkowski, Herbert. *Ways of Thought of Great Mathematicians*. San Francisco: Holden-Day, 1964.

Mikami, Y. *The Development of Mathematics in China and Japan*. New York: Chelsea House, 1974.

Motz, Lloyd, and Jefferson Weaver. *Conquering Mathematics*. New York: Plenum, 1991.

———. *The Story of Mathematics*. New York: Avon Books, 1993.

Newman, James. *The World of Mathematics*. New York: Simon & Schuster, 1966.

Ore, Oystein. *Number Theory and Its History*. New York: Dover, 1992.

Osen, Lynn. *Women in Mathematics*. Cambridge, MA: MIT Press, 1990.

Perl, Teri. *Math Equals: Biographies of Women Mathematicians*. Menlo Park, CA: Addison-Wesley, 1978.

Phillips, G. "Archimedes the Numerical Analyst." *American Mathematical Monthly* 88 (1981): 165–69.

Randall, John. *The Makings of the Modern Mind*. New York: Columbia University Press, 1976.

Reid, Constance. *From Zero to Infinity*. New York: Thomas Y. Crowell, 1985.

Reimer, Luetta, and Wilbert Reimer. *Mathematicians Are People, Too*. Palo Alto, CA: Dale Seymore, 1990.

Savant, Marilyn. *The World's Most Famous Math Problem*. New York: St. Martin's, 1993.

Scott, J. *A History of Mathematics*. Totowa, NJ: Barnes and Noble, 1975.

Smith, David. *The Hindu-Arabic Numerals*. Boston: Ginn, 1951.

———. *History of Mathematics*. (2 vols). New York: Dover, 1958.

Starr, Chester. *The Ancient Greeks*. New York: Oxford University Press, 1971.

Stewart, Ian. *Concepts of Modern Mathematics*. New York: Penguin, 1972.

———. *The Problems of Modern Mathematics*. Oxford, England: Oxford University Press, 1987.

———. *Does God Play Dice?* New York: Penguin Books, 1992.

Stonaker, Frances. *Famous Mathematicians*. New York: J. B. Lippincott, 1966.

Struik, Dirk. *A Concise History of Mathematics*, 4th ed. New York: Dover, 1987.

Szabo, A. *The Beginnings of Greek Mathematics*. Boston: Reidel, 1978.

Thomas, I. *Selections Illustrating the History of Greek Mathematics*. Cambridge, MA: Loeb Classical Library, 1941.

Turnbull, Herbert. *The Correspondence of Isaac Newton*. (7 vols). Cambridge, MA: Cambridge University Press, 1959–1977.

———. *The Great Mathematicians*. New York: New York University Press, 1981.

Vandiver, H. S. "Fermat's Last Theorem, Its History, and the Nature of the Known Results Concerning It." *American Mathematical Monthly* 83 (1976): 555–78.

Wade, Ira. "Women in Mathematics." *The Arithmetic Teacher* (April, 1970).

Westfall, R. S. *Never at Rest: A Biography of Isaac Newton*. Cambridge, MA: Cambridge University Press, 1980.

Whiteside, D. T. "Newton the Mathematician." *Contemporary Newtonian Research* 1 (1981): 179–388.

Index

About the Author

A former research scientist, Kendall Haven is the only West Point graduate to ever become a professional storyteller. He holds a Master's Degree in Oceanography and spent six years with the Department of Energy before finding his true passion for storytelling and a very different kind of "truth." He has performed for close to 3 million people, and won awards for his story-writing and storytelling. He has conducted workshops in over 20 states on storytelling's practical, in-class teaching power, and has become one of the nation's leading advocates for the educational value of storytelling.

Kendall has recorded audio tapes and published books of original stories. He has also used his writing talent to create stories for many non-profit organizations, including The American Cancer Society and the Institute for Mental Health Initiatives. He recently created a national award-winning adventure drama for National Public Radio on the effects of watching television.

Haven's most recent awards include the 1995 and 1996 Storytelling World Silver Award for best Story Anthology, the 1993 International Festival Association Silver Award for best Education Program, the 1992 Corporation for Public Broadcasting Silver Award for best Children's Public Radio Production, and the 1991 Award for Excellence in California Education. He has twice been an American Library Association "Notable Recording Artist," and is the only storyteller in the United States with three entries in the ALA's *Best of the Best for Children.*

Haven is founder and Chair of the International Whole Language Umbrella Storytelling Interest Group, and is on the Board of Directors as well as the Educational Advisory Committee of the National Storytelling Association. He is a co-director of the Sonoma Storytelling Festival, past four-year Chair of the Bay Area Storytelling Festival, and founder of storytelling festivals in Las Vegas, NV; Boise, ID; and Mariposa, CA.

He lives with his wife in the rolling Sonoma County grape vineyards in rural Northern California.